COMPLETE INTERVIEW PROCEDURES FOR HIRING SCHOOL PERSONNEL

WILLIAM L. GAGNON JR.

A SCARECROWEDUCATION BOOK

The Scarecrow Press, Inc.
Lanham, Maryland, and Oxford
2003

A SCARECROWEDUCATION BOOK

Published in the United States of America
by Scarecrow Press, Inc.
A Member of the Rowman & Littlefield Publishing Group
4720 Boston Way, Lanham, Maryland 20706
www.scarecroweducation.com

PO Box 317
Oxford OX2 9RU, UK

Copyright © 2003 by William L. Gagnon Jr.

All rights reserved. No part of this publication may be reproduced, stored
in a retrieval system, or transmitted in any form or by any means, electronic,
mechanical, photocopying, recording, or otherwise, without the prior permission
of the publisher.

British Library Cataloguing in Publication Information Available

Library of Congress Cataloging-in-Publication Data

Gagnon, William L., Jr., 1936–
  Complete interview procedures for hiring school personnel / William L.
Gagnon Jr.
     p. cm.
"A ScarecrowEducation book."
  ISBN 0-8108-4504-0 (pbk. : alk. paper)
  1. School employees—Selection and appointment. 2. Employment
interviewing. I. Title.
  LB2831.57.S45 G34 2003
  331.7'611371'01—dc21   2002009888

∞™ The paper used in this publication meets the minimum requirements of
American National Standard for Information Sciences—Permanence of Paper
for Printed Library Materials, ANSI/NISO Z39.48-1992.
Manufactured in the United States of America.

For Barbara

CONTENTS

CONTENTS

ACKNOWLEDGMENTS

My deepest appreciation is extended to my many friends who were kind enough to provide me with insight into specific academic disciplines. Their questions generated still more questions; their critique was both thought-provoking and awakening and their encouragement so important.

My experience as a director of human resources with both the East Hartford, Connecticut, public school and the Hicksville, New York, public schools provided me with unimaginable experiences, some of which I was able to incorporate into provocative questions. Upon retirement, my experience as an educational consultant, which included administrative searches and investigations of employee misconduct, provided me with still additional insights, all of which convinced me of the need for a manual such as this.

My deep appreciation is extended to the kind folks at Scarecrow Education who were so helpful, especially Tom Koerner, Christine Ambrose, and Laura Larson.

Thanks to all of the following for their suggested questions and assistance:

Louis Andurjar, Robert Brigockas, Nancy and Frank Burke, Robert Corso, Erland Cutter, Steven Edwards, Catherine Fenton, Anthony Fragola, Colette Gagnon, Mary Hogan, Jacqueline Jacoby, Robert Marchese, Sharon McQuade, Richard Mills, James O'Brien, Helene Padegimas, Lynne Pierson, Jack Pietrick, Tricia Royston, Richard Scanlan, Nancy Thorpe, David Title, and Thomas Yacavone.

I also extend my appreciation to Edward Byrne, my friend of forty-plus years, for proofreading the manuscript as well as for all of his comments and suggestions.

A very special thank you is extended to my wonderful wife, Barbara, for her suggestions, constant support, encouragement, and love.

INTRODUCTION

Most school districts do not have a full-time human resources administrator to conduct interviews; therefore, that important initial endeavor most often becomes the responsibility of the building principal or a department head. The task of conducting an interview may even be delegated to a person unfamiliar not only with the questioning process but with the academic discipline in which the vacancy occurs. In those situations, the interviewer is forced to perform under far less than favorable circumstances, and the interview often becomes counterproductive.

This book is designed to assist school administrators with the interview process by providing procedures and interview questions to be asked of candidates that are both appropriate and substantial. The procedures in Part One will provide the school district with guidelines for developing a hiring procedure policy. The over one thousand interview questions in forty-five employment categories will provide for a productive interview as well as spur other questions that will be pertinent to the vacancy and the demographics of that particular school district.

This book addresses various formats for conducting interviews and suggests activities to be conducted in addition to the usual questions. Basic guidelines are provided to assist the reader in examining résumés, checking references, and conducting interviews. Make every effort to improve these skills.

Persons using this manual are encouraged to examine the interview questions in categories of similar positions. Regardless of the teaching category, be certain to refer to the section entitled "General Questions for All Disciplines" as it provides significant generic questions. An effort has also been made to include more general material including chapters on "Classroom Management" and "The First-Year Teacher." Other areas, such as "Coach" and "Parent Volunteer," are positions too often overlooked in the interview process.

Above all, keep in mind that an interview is a two-way street. Not only are you interviewing the candidate, but the candidate is interviewing you. Both have to leave with a positive impression. Will this person fit? Will this person be happy? Is there a match? You may not always make the correct hiring decision, but this book will greatly improve your chances of hiring the best-qualified person.

THE INTERVIEW PROCESS

The school district has created a new position and begins the process to find a candidate. The unexpected resignation of a teacher arrives on the desk of the superintendent of schools. The position may be one where the availability of replacements is not a major concern, or it may be one where qualified teachers for that discipline are few and far between. In both cases, the school district needs to set in motion a procedure to evaluate its needs and to hire a qualified individual. To accomplish this properly, it will be necessary to evaluate several aspects of the hiring procedure.

The hiring procedure is not the responsibility of one individual. It always involves several people, and each will have an impact on how the district is viewed in the applicant's eyes. Some school employees, in fact, may not even know that they have been instrumental in a person's accepting or declining a job offer. The impact may be as simple as how a secretary answers a telephone question or the atmosphere in the interview room itself. It may be the appearance of the building when the candidate visits or an employee's offer of assistance to a stranger walking in the hallway. It may be the administrator who takes extra time to carefully read the candidate's vita as opposed to one who does a quick screening to determine which candidates are going to cost the school district less money.

The school district that takes the time to carefully formulate a hiring procedure for all employees will be successful in attracting and hiring responsible individuals.

1

IDENTIFYING THE POSITION

The Job Description

One of the most common errors made prior to advertising for a vacancy is the failure to identify the position properly. A school district will post and advertise a position, whether it is newly created or already exists and has become vacant, without first reviewing the job description (assuming there is one), to determine whether the qualifications are spelled out and the responsibilities are current. It seems ironic that this basic procedure is so often overlooked. A job description should exist for every position in the school district. The job description outlines the qualifications necessary to hold the position, the duties and responsibilities of the position, and it delineates any educational as well as special physical requirements that may be necessary for a person to be qualified for the position. The job description is the document against which evaluations are written and should be available for anyone to read upon request.

Many of us will spend hours determining exactly what kind of an automobile we anticipate purchasing. Will it be a SUV or a sedan? How many doors will it have? Air conditioning? Sunroof? Front-wheel drive? We begin our search only after we have determined the answers to such basic questions. Should we do less when hiring an employee?

Some basic questions are directly related to the job description that need to be answered prior to beginning a search to fill a vacant position. Professional staff questions may include the following:

What importance is placed on experience?
What special kinds of experience, such as working in an urban setting, are important?
What is the criteria concerning candidates with no experience but with otherwise promising credentials?
What are the public school criteria relative to candidates from parochial or private schools?
What is the minimum degree the candidate must have obtained?
What importance is placed on the college that awarded the degree?
What importance is placed on the candidate's college grades?
What kind of state certification or license is required for this position?
What importance is placed on candidates who hold dual certification in order to teach more than one subject?
What is the district's policy on actively seeking minority candidates?

Nonprofessional staff questions may include the following:

What is the minimum education requirement?
What specialized training or formal education is required in areas such as electrical work, secretarial work, or computer programming?
What state or municipality licenses are required for the position?
What kind of on-the-job experience is required?
What are the possibilities that this position will require direct contact with students?

CHAPTER 1

All positions may include the following considerations:

What physical requirements such as reaching, bending, lifting, pushing, or pulling are required for this position?

What expectations exist for working with hazardous materials?

What are the requirements for driving a vehicle?

What are the requirements for working with heavy equipment?

What are the requirements for working with dangerous equipment such as power tools, stoves, selected athletic equipment, or toxic chemicals?

Advertising for candidates and beginning the interview process should begin only after the district has considered all such requirements and has carefully reviewed the job description.

2

POSTING AND ADVERTISING THE VACANCY

The school district must have a procedure in place that outlines how and when a position will be posted (usually a document placed on a bulletin board at the work site) and advertised (usually in a newspaper or journal) should a vacancy occur. In most cases that requirement will be outlined in the language of the bargaining unit contract. If the position is not represented by a bargaining unit, language must be developed and placed in the school district's policy manual. In both cases, that language should clearly state the following:

The title of the position that is vacant
The starting date of work
The duties and responsibilities of the position
The salary
The application requirements and procedure
The deadline date for applications to be submitted

The language of bargaining unit contracts must be carefully examined to determine how an internal candidate (a current employee) will be evaluated as opposed to how someone not employed by the school district will be evaluated.

The posting will also outline the materials a candidate must submit when making application for the position, such as the following:

A cover letter
A formal application prepared by the school district that is completed and signed by the applicant
A current résumé
A listing of persons to be contacted for references and/or letters of reference
A copy of a valid certificate or license if required for the position
A copy of college transcripts if proof of education is required

In some cases, the district may require additional relevant materials for professional positions, such as these:

An essay on a specific subject
A copy of published articles

CHAPTER 2

A portfolio
A videotape of the candidate teaching a class

Most school districts will and should require that all of the requested materials must be submitted in order for the application to be considered complete and ready for review. The school district should make it clear that incomplete vitae will not be considered.

3

SCREENING THE CANDIDATE'S VITAE

Upon receiving the required documents, the interviewer will need to conduct a careful examination of the candidate's vitae. This is an extremely important process for it will determine which candidates are selected for an interview.

THE COVER LETTER

Check the letter for general appearance. Does it meet the expectations of the position? (Don't expect to see the same qualities in a letter from a candidate with a Ph.D. as opposed to a candidate who has not finished high school.) Are there any misspellings? Is the letter grammatically correct? Has the letter been signed?

On occasion, applicants will use a standard letter that is stored in a word processor software program but will forget to change the name of the school district they are sending it to. Don't be surprised to find a letter addressed to a school district other than the one intended. This error is happening too frequently.

Some candidates prefer to write a short cover letter stating only that they are applying for the position. Others will write a lengthy cover letter highlighting much of the information that is provided in the résumé. Either format is acceptable, but the longer letter should not exceed one page.

Candidates often submit a cover letter on colored paper. This is done with the hope that the letter will stand out. Some, usually candidates for primary grades, will use paper decorated with toys or educational symbols. Put all of those things aside and concentrate on the written content of the letter.

THE RÉSUMÉ

The most important section to check on a résumé is the candidate's employment history. If you note an unexplained employment time lapse, your suspicion should be automatically aroused. Such a gap will need to be carefully examined. Ask yourself why. There is always a reason, usually of a serious nature, why employment years have been omitted on a résumé.

Once you are satisfied that the work history is complete, go back to the job description to check the required criteria and examine the résumé to see whether those requirements have been completed.

A résumé does not have to be lengthy; in fact, human resource administrators will attest that most résumés can be outlined on a single piece of paper. A résumé should point out aspects of the candidate's career that can be examined further in the interview. Résumés that cover several pages have a tendency not to be read thoroughly.

Keep in mind that a first-year teacher, just graduated from college, will be looking for material to add to the résumé. It will be important to go beyond the résumé for these candidates, and the letters of reference may be the most important evaluative tool.

CHAPTER 3

THE CERTIFICATION AND LICENSES

Check to be certain the dates are valid and the document satisfies the requirement of the job description. When teachers and administrators are moving from a different state, the certification may not be valid, but an agreement of reciprocity may exist between states. That will need to be clarified with the state bureau of certification.

THE REFERENCES

Checking references is, without question, the most difficult part of the hiring process. It stands to reason that the candidate will not ask a person to write a letter of reference unless he or she knows that the letter will be positive. Fortunately, exceptions to that assumption often surface. Read the letters of reference very carefully, and read between the lines. What is the writer really saying? Which adjectives are used? Does the writer recommend, highly recommend, or recommend without reservation? Does the writer compare or rank this candidate with others? Does the writer give examples of how this candidate is exemplary? If the person has worked with children, does the writer cover this aspect? Is the writer a personal friend or a professional colleague? Does the writer offer to be available for further comment should the school district wish to telephone? If so, is there an implied negative message making a telephone call advisable?

A labor attorney will advise the school district to investigate references carefully, but that same attorney will advise the writer of the reference letter to be very careful what is conveyed either in writing or orally. There is always the danger of litigation if the candidate is rejected due to negative comments given in a reference letter or verbal communication.

References are usually checked after the candidate has been interviewed and is being considered as a finalist for the position. When that time comes, inform the candidate that you will be calling the persons identified as references as he or she may not have told those persons about seeking other employment.

Don't rely entirely on the candidate's current employer to obtain references. Check with supervisors and colleagues from the previous place of employment as these individuals may feel more free to express an honest opinion of the candidate you are considering for hire.

THE TRANSCRIPTS

Check to see that the diploma or degree awarded conforms to the résumé. If the school district has determined that grades are important, check the quality point ratio and grades for individual courses, especially those that deal with subjects to be taught. To save the school district time, accept unofficial copies of transcripts with the initial application with the understanding that official copies will be required should the position be offered.

SELECTING THE CANDIDATES TO BE INTERVIEWED

Begin this process by examining all of the applications for a vacancy without interruption. The initial reaction to the documents will be very important.

After reading the first candidate's vitae, be prepared to make an initial evaluation. One method of doing this is to place the candidate's vitae into one of three groups: "Valid Candidate," "Possible Candidate," and "No Further Interest." Move on to the next candidate and repeat the entire process. When all of the candidates' vitae have been evaluated, return to the candidates you initially identified in the "Possible Candidate" group, and determine whether that paperwork will be moved to one of the other two categories.

The candidates to interview for the vacancy have now been selected.

4

CONDUCTING CRIMINAL BACKGROUND CHECKS

Many states now require some form of criminal background check of public school employees. Some states require that this be done only for new employees. Other states either permit or require background checks for new or existing employees. Fingerprinting is the most common method of conducting a background check.

The fingerprints are sent to the state police and to the Federal Bureau of Investigation. A report is sent to the school district indicating either a negative history or a listing of felony convictions. The report from the FBI will also include any military convictions and, if applicable, an alias the person may have used.

The debate over to fingerprint or not to fingerprint is strong. In Maine, where existing staff must be fingerprinted, veteran teachers have left the profession over principle rather than be fingerprinted. In Connecticut, candidates have left the interview rather than be fingerprinted. Because it can take months to receive a fingerprint report, do we allow the individual to begin work before the report is received?

Are background checks worth the effort? Are they an invasion of privacy or unconstitutional? Has the procedure been effective detecting felons who are now working with or around children? Do all detected felons present a danger to students? Are school districts using this information in a manner not intended? How do we deal with an employee who becomes a felon *after* being fingerprinted?

The answers to these questions may appear to be obvious but are in fact complicated. If a person is a convicted felon, but the crime has nothing to do with children, is this enough of a reason to dismiss or not employ? Should a teacher, bookkeeper, or custodian be denied employment due to a conviction for civil disobedience that occurred while a college student fifteen years ago? At what point has a debt to society been paid?

Although not all felons may present a danger to children, teachers are role models, and that point must be taken into consideration. School districts must take every possible precaution to protect children. The school district does not want a convicted pedophile working with children or a convicted bank robber in charge of security, for example.

These are complicated issues that face every school district. Policy must be developed and guidelines completely understood by those in a position to hire.

5

DETERMINING THE TYPE
OF INTERVIEW

Different positions require different types of interviews. Obviously, a different procedure will be used for a top administrative position than for that of a classroom teacher. But will the procedure be different for a teacher as opposed to a nurse, secretary, or paraprofessional? For that matter, will the school district even conduct a formal interview when looking to hire a coach or a substitute teacher? The answer should unequivocally be yes! Absolutely no one, regardless of the position, should be hired or allowed to work or volunteer without a formal interview. That procedure provides protection for the person who hires, for the school district, and, most important, for the safety of all the children in the school district.

It is an important responsibility of the interviewer to create a pleasant and nonthreatening atmosphere for the interview. The interviewer must create an atmosphere in which the candidate will be at his or her best. Consider the following recommendations:

- Conduct the interview in a nonintimidating room with consideration to both size and surroundings. Be certain that the phone will not ring and that someone will not enter unexpectedly. Don't let a window be a distraction. Set a comfortable temperature for the room.
- Greet the candidate where he or she is waiting rather than having the person ushered in the room by a secretary. This will set a welcoming tone not missed by the candidate.
- Move from behind an authoritative desk to chairs around a table. The candidate is well aware who is in charge.

There are various interview formats to consider. The choice will obviously be influenced by the position.

THE TEN-MINUTE INTERVIEW

One of the most frustrating aspects of conducting interviews is a lack of time when there are many candidates. Only a handful of candidates are selected for an interview because of this time restraint. Unfortunately, it often becomes only too obvious, as little as five minutes into the interview, that some of the candidates selected are not going to be hired. Yet a half-hour of interview time still remains. The interviewer has no choice but to continue with the interview although there is only a slim possibility that the initial negative opinion will be changed. The Ten-Minute Interview is designed to assist with this awkward but realistic happening.

To develop a Ten-Minute Interview procedure, begin by mailing a letter not only to those candidates identified as promising but to those considered as marginal. Inform them that the school district is interested in scheduling an interview and that the meeting will not exceed ten minutes in length. Explain that this format is intended as an extension of the paper screening and that following these interviews, candidates from the group interviewed will be selected to return for a longer, formal traditional interview. Serious candidates will understand and will respond favorably. Very few will decline.

CHAPTER 5

Select up to three challenging questions for the interview, and be certain that the interview does not exceed ten minutes. In two hours, twelve candidates will have been interviewed rather than four for thirty minutes each, and the two hours spent interviewing will be much more productive. It will become clear very quickly which candidates to invite for a second interview, and the time spent will be more productive for the school district and more honest and fair to the candidate.

THE ONE-ON-ONE INTERVIEW

The most traditional form of interviewing is the one-on-one interview. The person hiring will meet with the candidate one-on-one, and the evaluation will be solely that of the interviewer.

A good variation on this procedure is to invite a second person to participate in the interview. One person cannot know all there is to know about the numerous positions in a school district. It simply is not possible to know all of this information. Yet it is important to know whether the candidate is giving valid answers to the questions asked. Invite a person with more expertise in the position to join you for the interview. This will be most beneficial when asking specific questions. If the interviewer is a building principal and is interviewing candidates for a music position but has little or no musical experience, invite a district music teacher to assist with the interview. If the interview is for a custodian position, find someone in the district with a good knowledge of electrical systems, hazardous materials, swimming pool maintenance, or resurfacing of floors to assist. For a foreign language position, bring in someone who can speak with the candidate in the language to be taught. An opening for a secretary? Invite another secretary who will be working side-by-side with this individual to assist.

THE COMMITTEE INTERVIEW

This format, traditionally used for administrative positions, is also being used more often for teaching positions. A committee of as few as six to as many as fifteen individuals, composed of teachers and administrators, may be selected. Depending on the position, the committee will often also include parents, board of education members, and even students. The candidate is scheduled for an interview of from thirty to forty-five minutes, and most members have the opportunity to ask one planned question. Following the interviews, the group evaluates the candidates and makes its recommendations.

A variation of this procedure is to divide the group into two committees and the candidate appears before each. One committee may ask questions dealing only with one topic, such as curriculum, whereas the other committee may ask more general questions. Or maybe the candidate will appear before three or four committees. A committee of parents or a committee of bargaining unit representatives may be suitable for certain positions in the district. Using this format, it is possible to schedule two or more candidates at the same time, rotating them between committees. This format allows the school district to interview more candidates for longer periods of time in the same number of clock hours.

When the committee format is used, it is important for one person to act as a host. That person should meet with the candidate prior to beginning the interview, informing him or her of the process to be used, how many persons will be in the room, how the candidate will be introduced, and how many questions will be asked. To help the candidate determine the length of responses to questions (because many do tend to speak at length), inform the candidate how much time has been allotted for the interview. If the candidate has handouts, the host can obtain these and distribute them to the committee. Inform the candidate whether questions will be allowed prior to his or her departure. Finally, the candidate should be given an opportunity to ask the host questions so that the procedure is clear prior to his or her entering the interview room.

6

USING WARM-UP QUESTIONS

All candidates have a degree of nervousness at the beginning of an interview. The interviewer needs to understand this fact and make every effort to relax the candidate. Perhaps the interviewer is familiar with the candidate's town and can comment on visiting there. Comment on the quality and reputation of his or her alma mater. Or ask, "Did you have any problem locating our office?" The amount of time allotted for an interview is short and moves quickly, so do not spend a great deal of time with this warm-up portion.

Additionally, to help the candidate settle down and feel comfortable, it is advisable that the first one or two questions be nonthreatening, such as the following:

- We have had an opportunity to examine your résumé. Please highlight those aspects of your career that directly relate to this position.
- Please briefly summarize your résumé.
- Please tell us what you know about our school district and why this position interests you.
- Please tell us about your current position and what you enjoy most about it.

7

PROVIDING PLANNED MATERIALS

In many cases, it is possible to provide the candidate with materials prior to the interview. Examples of such possibilities are given throughout the second section of this book dealing with interview questions. Some are as follows:

- If a person will be working with the budget, mail the candidate a copy of the district's budget a week ahead of time, and ask the candidate to come prepared to comment on the document.
- Mail copies of the curriculum to a teaching candidate; ask him or her to come prepared to comment on the documents.
- Mail a copy of the student handbook to the candidate for an assistant principal position, asking him or her to come prepared to comment on the document.
- Mail elementary teacher candidates copies of three actual student essays: one considered to be very good, one considered good, and one considered unsatisfactory. Ask the candidate to come prepared to discuss these three essays. Do not forget to delete the student names prior to mailing, however.
- Mail the building maintenance schedule to the candidate for a head custodian position, and ask the candidate to come prepared to comment on the procedure.

8

REQUIRING CANDIDATES TO TEACH

The single most important planning the school district can undertake for teacher candidates is to inform them that they will be required to teach a lesson to one of the district's classes that will be both videotaped and observed by the interview team. Teachers are the most important employees of the school district—that point is not debatable. A school district must do everything in its power to hire only the best-qualified candidates. Their credentials are examined. They are interviewed extensively. Their references are checked. In spite of all of this, the school district has no firsthand knowledge whether they can do what they are hired to do. The school district does not know until after they are hired and in charge of a classroom of students whether they can teach. This makes no sense! Yet the remedy is so simple. Before hiring, observe the candidate teaching a class.

9

SELECTING THE
INTERVIEW QUESTIONS

The second section of this book contains over one thousand interview questions in forty-eight employment areas in education. Use these as written, or modify them to meet the school district's needs. The interviewer is encouraged to use more than one category of questions for each discipline.

The following points are important when interviewing more than one candidate for the same position:

- Ask the same questions, and only those questions, of all the candidates.
- Ask the question the same way each time. Don't improvise.
- Ask a follow-up question if the candidate piques your interest with his or her response.
- Ask the same questions of an in-house candidate as of those from outside the district.

ANSWERING THE CANDIDATE'S QUESTIONS

There is debate on whether to provide time for a candidate to ask questions prior to his or her departure. The interview, after all, is a two-way proposition. While the candidate is being evaluated by those in a position to hire, the candidate unquestionably is also evaluating the district through the persons who are asking the questions.

Some believe it is important to provide time prior to the end of the interview for the candidate to ask questions. The problem with allowing questions is that this may be premature if the interviewer knows there is no chance of this candidate moving forward in the hiring process. Additionally, some candidates ask questions that pertain to employment contracts that cannot be answered at that time. Some candidates will ask too many questions, and doing so presents a real danger that an initial positive impression by the interviewer may change to a negative one.

An alternative is to explain to the candidate that this is a preliminary interview and that several people are being seen; consequently, the candidates will not be given time to ask questions. However, if invited back for a second interview, time will be provided for the candidate's questions at that second interview.

EVALUATING THE INTERVIEW

Design an evaluation sheet to be used for all interviews that every person who adjudicates the interview process would be required to complete. Keep it simple. Use as few topics for evaluation as possible, and evaluate each of these in categories such as outstanding, very good, good, acceptable, and poor. Leave room in each category for written comments. Among the categories to include on the evaluation sheet are the following:

Knowledge of subject area
Verbal/communication skills
Ability to respond to questions
Clarity
Creativity
Appearance and poise
Comfort level
Overall reaction to candidate

Rather than judging each of these areas with the terms suggested in the previous paragraph, many school districts prefer to award a numerical grade, adding the grade in each category for a final evaluation of the candidate. All of the candidates are then placed in numerical order. That procedure can be very dangerous for it does not leave room for the subjective evaluation. Does the candidate with the highest score automatically get hired? If so, is he or she really the best candidate for the school district? Is it possible that a candidate with a lower score will be a better fit within the school community? Is it necessary for the interview committee to even discuss the candidates if the outcome is determined by a numerical grade? Numerically ranking the candidates also ties the hands of the person who must make the final decision on who is to be hired. Finally, does this procedure leave the school district subject to litigation should the person with the highest score not be hired?

After hearing all of the interviews, allow the committee time to openly discuss the candidates. If at all possible, avoid having the critique session turn into a debate. Ask each committee member, one at a time, to tell others about the pros and cons of each candidate, what they liked and did not like. Ask each committee member to conclude his or her critique by selecting the top three to be moved forward in the hiring procedure. After each committee member has spoken, a consensus will be obvious and the interview process completed.

The choice has been made. Depending on the position, the top candidate will be hired or the top three candidates will be moved forward in the hiring process, perhaps to next meet with the superintendent of schools.

12

EVALUATING THE PROCEDURE

Evaluate your entire hiring procedure often. Constant evaluation will improve the hiring procedure, which, in turn, will improve the quality of person hired in the school district.

An additional evaluative tool is to design a questionnaire to be completed by successful candidates. You can also mail this form to unsuccessful candidates, but don't expect a large response. Ironically, it is the unsuccessful candidate who may provide you with the most honest evaluation of your process. The questionnaire should have a rating scale, provide an opportunity for written comments, and ask questions such as the following:

How would you rate the school district's application process response time?

Were you treated in a professional manner by the office staff?

What is your reaction to the Ten-Minute Interview process?

Were you made to feel welcome when you began the interview?

Was the interview committee properly introduced?

Did you feel intimidated during the interview process?

Were the interview questions relevant to the vacancy/position?

Were you provided with enough time to fully answer the questions?

Was the response time between the interview and notification of the committee's decision reasonable?

OVER ONE THOUSAND INTERVIEW QUESTIONS IN FORTY-FIVE EMPLOYMENT AREAS TO ASK THE CANDIDATES

INTERVIEW NOTES FOR SUPERINTENDENT OF SCHOOLS

Interview Date   Candidate(s) Interviewed   Questions Used

Notes/Additional Questions

SUPERINTENDENT OF SCHOOLS

1. Why do you aspire to be a superintendent?
2. Please tell us the three most important attributes that qualify you for this position.
3. Please tell us about your most difficult administrative predicament—how you handled it and how you arrived at your decision.
4. Please tell us about a specific difficult situation you handled concerning a staff member.
5. Please tell us about a specific rewarding experience in your educational career.
6. What is your experience with developing a district school budget?
7. Other than there never being enough money, what is the single most difficult problem in developing a district school budget?
8. How do you prioritize cutting the budget in the development stage?
9. Have you had experience with grant writing?
10. What kinds of experiences have you had with building construction projects?
11. What kinds of experiences have you had with bargaining units?
12. What kinds of experiences have you had with bargaining unit contract negotiations?
13. What kinds of experiences have you had with bus transportation companies?
14. What kinds of experiences have you had with food services companies?
15. What kinds of experiences have you had with town/city elected officials?
16. What would be your three most important personal expectations if you were to be appointed superintendent?
17. You have worked in this school system for [*insert*] years and know many of the staff personally. Will that have any bearing on how you conduct business?
18. You are new to our district and have been provided with materials concerning us. What have you learned from that material that both pleases and disturbs you?
19. What are your expectations from the board of education?
20. How informed do you plan to keep the board of education?
21. Are there times when the board of education should not be given immediate information?
22. Would you object to individual board members approaching staff to obtain information?
23. Have you had any experience dealing with parochial and/or other private schools?
24. How would you organize and utilize your immediate central office staff?
25. What expectations would you have for the assistant superintendent?

INTERVIEW NOTES FOR ASSISTANT SUPERINTENDENT OF SCHOOLS

Interview Date   Candidate(s) Interviewed   Questions Used

Notes/Additional Questions

14

ASSISTANT SUPERINTENDENT
OF SCHOOLS

1. What personal attributes are important for a person to succeed as an assistant superintendent?
2. Please tell us which specific position you have held that best prepared you to be an assistant superintendent.
3. What do you consider as a weakness in your background for this position?
4. What functions do you consider yourself well prepared for should they be assigned to you in this position?
5. Please talk to us about your experience with budget preparation.
6. Where would you look first if it became necessary to recommend cutting the budget?
7. Do you have experience with grant applications?
8. What procedure would you use for the yearly evaluation of building principals?
9. What procedure would you use should you find a district administrator incompetent yet protected by tenure?
10. What is the role of parent organizations?
11. How would you work with parent organizations?
12. What are your views concerning student field trips?
13. What are your views concerning out-of-state student field trips?
14. What are your views concerning staff development?
15. Why do we often hear that staff development is not beneficial?
16. Teachers always state they do not have enough time in a school day yet are often absent to attend staff development meetings or a workshop. How do you reconcile these approaches?
17. Please talk to us about your leadership skills as they pertain to curriculum, supervision, and staff development.
18. How would you handle proposed changes to the curriculum?
19. Please talk to us about standardized testing.
20. What steps would you take to improve standardized test scores?
21. Do you have any preschool curriculum experience?
22. Would you expect to have a role in the selection of new teachers?
23. Do you have any experience dealing with the public media including, but not limited to, press releases and being interviewed personally?
24. How would you handle a philosophical disagreement with the superintendent?
25. Do you aspire to be a superintendent in your professional career?

INTERVIEW NOTES FOR DIRECTOR OF CURRICULUM/INSTRUCTION

Interview Date   Candidate(s) Interviewed   Questions Used

Notes/Additional Questions

15

DIRECTOR OF CURRICULUM/INSTRUCTION

1. What constitutes quality instruction?
2. What are your minimum expectations when you observe a classroom?
3. What do you believe to be the principal duties of this position if you are appointed?
4. What instructional practices should be standardized between buildings with similar grade levels?
5. How would you go about assessing the curriculum that is in place?
6. How would you go about assessing curriculum development?
7. What do you believe to be the authoritative relationship between the director of instruction and building principals?
8. What curriculum changes did you initiate in your previous position?
9. How would you go about instituting curriculum change?
10. In which curricula are you most comfortable conducting a workshop?
11. How would you deal with a teacher who does not believe in a curriculum change that has been made and continues to reject new initiatives?
12. What steps would you take to improve a marginal teacher?
13. What do you do when you determine that a marginal teacher will never be better than marginal?
14. What steps would you take if a group of teachers approached you about a department head not providing the necessary leadership to improve instruction in that department?
15. Please talk to us about your views concerning standardized testing.
16. What are your views on retaining students at grade level for a second year?
17. Please describe your beliefs concerning textbook selection.
18. Please discuss the use of computers in the classroom.
19. Do you prefer computers being placed in the classroom or in a laboratory setting?
20. Teachers are constantly complaining that they are required to cover more additional material but that there are only so many minutes in a day for instruction. How do you answer those complaints?
21. How would you deal with the concept of pullout programs?
22. What are your beliefs concerning homework?
23. What are your beliefs concerning half-day or full-day kindergarten?
24. What are your beliefs concerning the visual and performing arts being scheduled during the school day?
25. How would you approach the area of vocational education?

INTERVIEW NOTES FOR DIRECTOR OF HUMAN RESOURCES

Interview Date   Candidate(s) Interviewed   Questions Used

Notes/Additional Questions

16

DIRECTOR OF HUMAN RESOURCES

1. Please share with us your plans for the hiring process in our district.
2. What is the role of the director of human resources in the hiring process?
3. What constitutes a good interview?
4. What do you look for during an interview?
5. In your experience as the interviewer, how often have you changed your opinion of the candidate after the first few minutes of the interview?
6. Should the board of education have a role in hiring teachers?
7. How would you resolve a conflict between two administrators on a hiring recommendation?
8. How much input should a building principal have in selecting the teaching staff?
9. Should parents have a role in the teacher hiring process?
10. What qualities will you be looking for when hiring an administrator?
11. What do you look for in a résumé?
12. How do you know that references are honest?
13. What is your opinion on the fingerprinting of employees?
14. How do we protect our students from employee candidates who perhaps should not be working with children?
15. Certain disciplines are experiencing a major shortage of teachers. How will you be able to hire qualified teachers as long as this problem exists?
16. Do you have any suggestions on how to recruit minority teachers?
17. How would you screen candidates for substitute teacher positions?
18. Please summarize your experience with organized labor either as a current or past member or within your experience working with a bargaining unit.
19. How do you view the role of organized labor relative to professional organizations?
20. Have you had any experience negotiating bargaining unit contracts?
21. How do you approach the entire process when you begin to plan for contract negotiations?
22. What are some of the dangerous oversights in setting ground rules for contract negotiations?
23. In contract negotiations, both sides tend to include language in their proposals that they are willing to forsake at some point in the process. Why not simply present an honest package?
24. Regardless of the bargaining group, what are some financial as well as nonfinancial areas that the administration should address and why?
25. Please tell us about your experience with the grievance procedure.
26. Please tell us about a sensitive grievance that you were involved in. How did you handle it? What was the outcome?
27. How much should we base our contract negotiations on existing contracts of neighboring school districts?

CHAPTER 16

28. When hearing a grievance for the administration, how do you separate the implied contract language from the actual language?

29. When hearing a grievance for the administration, how do you separate the contract language from the personal emotions that often accompany such a process?

30. When initially examining a grievance, what elements are you looking for to ascertain the merit of the grievance?

31. Does knowing full well that a grievance will be filed at a higher level, should it be denied, have any bearing on your decision to grant or deny?

32. Please tell us under what circumstances you may advise a district administrator not to proceed with a proposed grievance.

33. If a principal were to come to you and ask that a teacher be placed on some sort of extended evaluation for alleged incompetence, what are some of the basic questions you would initially ask that principal?

34. Do you have experience with the arbitration process?

35. Please tell us about your experience testifying at state labor/arbitration department hearings.

36. Once a grievance goes to arbitration, would you continue to take steps to achieve a settlement?

37. Do you have any suggestions on how to make peace with a bargaining unit that has a long history of conflict between that unit and the administration?

38. What steps would you take to become acquainted with our bargaining units if you were appointed to this position?

39. What is your opinion of teacher tenure?

40. What steps would you put in place to lower the possibility of an inferior teacher attaining tenure?

41. Is it possible to terminate an inferior teacher?

42. Do you have experience in the administration of employee benefits?

43. Do you have experience in the administration of employee medical benefits?

44. Do you have experience in the administration of major medical programs?

45. Prior to coming to today's interview, we asked you to examine our medical benefits program in order to give us your views both pro and con. Please do so at this time.

46. What is the depth of your experience with workers' compensation programs?

47. How would you investigate alleged employee abuse of workers' compensation?

48. Do you have experience working with the Family Medical Leave Act (FMLA)?

49. Please give us an example of a possible conflict between FMLA and bargaining unit contract language and how the conflict would be resolved.

50. What is your understanding of FMLA legislation should a male teacher request a child-rearing leave?

51. Do you have experience working with the Americans with Disabilities Act (ADA)?

52. Have you had any experience dealing with employee alcohol or drug abuse under ADA or FMLA legislation? If so, please give us an example of how you handled the situation and the outcome.

53. Have you had any experience dealing with allegations of child abuse? If so, please give us an example of how you handled the situation and the outcome.

54. What steps would you immediately take should you receive an allegation of child abuse by an employee?

55. Do you have experience working with Title IX?

56. What is your experience with computerized programs for handling the work of a human resources office?

57. What instructions would you give to your office personnel relative to your expectations for dealing with the public?

58. What do you believe are the three most often heard complaints by employees as related to the human resources department, and how would you remedy each of these?

59. Have you ever developed a personnel budget for a school district?

60. When you don't know how many teachers will retire in a given year or how many new sections of elementary grades you may require, how do you go about establishing a justifiable personnel budget?

NOTES

INTERVIEW NOTES FOR BUSINESS MANAGER

Interview Date   Candidate(s) Interviewed   Questions Used

Notes/Additional Questions

BUSINESS MANAGER

1. What specific experiences in your background make you qualified to be a school business manager?
2. We sent you a copy of our current school budget and asked that you come prepared to offer your observations. Please do so at this time.
3. What changes would you make concerning our school budget procedures?
4. How do you view the relationship of the business manager with the superintendent of schools and the board of education?
5. How would you organize the staffing of a school business department?
6. Are you familiar with any of the required state reports filed by the business department?
7. Do you have experience with electronic filing of state reports?
8. What purchase order procedures would you put in place?
9. How would you coordinate the purchase of supplies for our schools?
10. Would there be a method for making a purchase without a purchase order in an emergency situation?
11. Would you permit teachers to purchase supplies at an office supply store and be reimbursed?
12. Who should be permitted to use a district credit card?
13. What reports would you regularly make to the board of education, and what format would they take?
14. It is November 1, and spending has exceeded expectations. What steps would you immediately take?
15. An administrator has purchased new furniture without an approved purchase order because it was allocated in the budget. How would you handle such a situation?
16. How would you administrate student activity accounts?
17. How should gate revenues at an athletic event be handled?
18. How would you administrate petty cash accounts?
19. What is a reasonable amount of money for a building petty cash account?
20. Your responsibilities will also include administration of the employee benefits program. What experience have you had in this area?
21. How can we cut employee benefit costs?
22. How do we know employee benefit accounts are not being abused?
23. We are currently negotiating bargaining unit contracts. What advice would you give concerning language dealing with employee benefits?
24. What experience have you had with unemployment compensation?
25. How would you handle allegations of abuse of unemployment compensation claims?

INTERVIEW NOTES FOR DIRECTOR OF PUPIL PERSONNEL SERVICES/SPECIAL EDUCATION

Interview Date   Candidate(s) Interviewed   Questions Used

Notes/Additional Questions

18

DIRECTOR OF PUPIL PERSONNEL SERVICES/SPECIAL EDUCATION

1. What are the strengths and weaknesses of inclusion?
2. How would you develop an inclusion program for [*select an age and disability*], and how would you go about implementing such a program, including curriculum and budget?
3. What is the role of the building principal in relation to the director of special education's role where special education inclusion programs are concerned?
4. How do you handle the reluctant parents when they disagree with your inclusion plan?
5. How does the director know whether the inclusion plan is working?
6. An emotionally disturbed student moves into your district. The student has been attending a private special education school at an approximate cost of $30,000 per year. The parents wish to continue this placement. How would you handle this situation?
7. What would you do to reduce out-of-district placement costs?
8. Should local students remain within the district rather than being placed out of district if at all possible?
9. How would you work with parents relative to in-district or out-of-district placements?
10. Under what circumstances should parents force a district into an out-of-district placement?
11. What is the extent of your experience in developing special education budgets?
12. State statutes mandate extremely high special education budgets. If you were making a presentation to the board of education on this topic, what would you say to them in support of these expenditures?
13. The approved district budget provides a specific amount of money for supplies, textbooks, and instruction. How do you divide the funds evenly among grade levels?
14. How do you determine whether or not teachers really need more money?
15. How would you assess your special education programs in relationship to spending?
16. What state and federal programs are available to help with district funding, and how would you use these?
17. When hiring a new teacher, what qualities are important to you?
18. How do you determine if a teacher is better suited for a one-on-one or traditional classroom assignment?
19. How do you deal with the parent who demands that the child be moved to a different teacher?
20. Please share with us your expectations for paraprofessionals assigned to the special education department.
21. What qualities are important to look for when hiring a paraprofessional who will be dealing with a one-on-one placement?
22. How would you handle friction that has developed between a teacher and the paraprofessional assigned to his or her class?
23. Talk about the dilemma we know exists between the paraprofessional who, against the law, actually teaches as opposed to reinforcing the lessons of the teacher?
24. How would you handle a breach of confidentiality by a member of your staff?
25. What in-service programs would you either plan or want to see your staff attend?
26. What are your expectations relative to teaching reading, for example, within the special education program?

CHAPTER 18

27. What are your expectations relative to the availability of the assigned teachers within a building in areas such as music, art, and physical education, as related to special education?
28. What in your mind constitutes a collaborative model?
29. What is the first thing you do when informed of allegations of child abuse?
30. How would you conduct an investigation involving allegations of child abuse?
31. How do you normally respond to an inquiry from the Department of Children and Family Services?
32. How do you assess when a special education program is working?
33. What constitutes a "good special education teacher"?
34. What constitutes "good special education instruction"?
35. How do you evaluate quality special education instruction?
36. Please give us an example of a successful class or program you have observed and why it was working.
37. What constitutes a good pupil placement team (PPT)?
38. Does an effective PPT really require so many persons to participate?
39. How would you deal with a staff member who very often is not cooperative regarding PPTs and cites "personal scheduling conflicts" as a reason for noncooperation?
40. What general characteristic do you find lacking in a first-year special education teacher, and what would you do to correct that deficiency?

NOTES

INTERVIEW NOTES FOR DIRECTOR OF COMPUTER/TECHNOLOGY SERVICES

Interview Date   Candidate(s) Interviewed   Questions Used

Notes/Additional Questions

19

DIRECTOR OF COMPUTER/TECHNOLOGY SERVICES

1. Please discuss the pros and cons of PCs versus Macintosh computers in the classroom.
2. Why should students learn to use computers on a Mac when the business world uses PCs?
3. Please discuss the pros and cons of placing computers at the elementary school level in classrooms or in a laboratory setting.
4. Please summarize a recent workshop you conducted for a teaching staff.
5. What should be the school district's minimum expectation of a teacher's computer expertise?
6. What is your opinion of providing laptops to all students in grade 7, for example?
7. Please discuss safeguards in terms of students downloading Internet material.
8. What is your experience in developing district technology budgets?
9. What percentage of your budget would be designated for software?
10. You were provided with information detailing the district's current level of technology. What would you designate as priorities if you were appointed to this position?
11. What procedures would you establish for the selection and purchase of software?
12. Considering the size of our school district, how would you determine whether hardware repairs should be done in-house or through a contracted service?
13. Are you familiar with any software programs that can be used for district administrative purposes?
14. Our school district needs to connect all of our building and the administrative office computers. What is your experience in this area?
15. If you were to be appointed to this position, what immediate steps would you take to evaluate the school district's current level of technology efficiency?

INTERVIEW NOTES FOR DIRECTOR OF PLANT OPERATIONS

Interview Date   Candidate(s) Interviewed   Questions Used

Notes/Additional Questions

20

DIRECTOR OF PLANT OPERATIONS

1. What specific experiences do you have to qualify you for this position?
2. Which trades are you adequate in supervising?
3. Is it cost-effective to hire tradespeople rather than contract for such services?
4. Our district employs carpenters, electricians, plumbers, and general maintainers. These people often work in buildings while school is in session. What guidelines would you give such employees when hired?
5. This is a small district, and you would be required to do maintenance repairs in addition to supervision. How would you organize your day to accommodate both functions?
6. How would you organize repair requests?
7. How do you deal with the principal who calls very often with an "urgent" request?
8. What experience have you had in developing budgets?
9. How would you handle an emergency expenditure that was not included in the budget?
10. Have you ever developed capital improvement projects?
11. What kinds of projects are usually included in capital improvement projects?
12. Have you ever prepared and/or evaluated construction bids?
13. What qualities would you look for when hiring a school custodian?
14. What expectations should we have of our school custodians?
15. Several teachers in one building complain that the custodian is not cleaning the rooms to their satisfaction. How would you handle such a complaint?
16. How would you handle a suspicion of theft by a custodian?
17. How would you deal with a custodian who is constantly absent under workers' compensation?
18. What is your experience dealing with hazardous materials?
19. What precautions would you put in place concerning hazardous materials?
20. Have you ever worked in a supervisory position where a bargaining unit represented the employees?
21. Have you ever had to adjudicate grievances?
22. How do you evaluate a grievance?
23. Please give us an example of a grievance you found to be justified and how you handled the situation.
24. Please give us an example of a disciplinary action you took against an employee.
25. After assigning a work order to a tradesperson, you determine that the job is taking far too long to complete. How would you handle such a situation?

INTERVIEW NOTES FOR PRINCIPAL OF ELEMENTARY SCHOOL

Interview Date   Candidate(s) Interviewed   Questions Used

Notes/Additional Questions

21

PRINCIPAL OF ELEMENTARY SCHOOL

1. Please tell us when in your career you made the decision to aspire to be a principal and why.
2. What constitutes quality instruction?
3. Are there new trends in instruction that excite you and that you would propose to the faculty if you were to be appointed principal?
4. Please tell this committee what you believe constitutes the broad term of *technology in education* as well as your beliefs on the use of technology in today's elementary schools.
5. What is your opinion of standardized testing?
6. Should the principal be concerned about how often the classroom teacher tests students?
7. Please address the issue of class size and heterogeneity.
8. School safety has become a major concern in today's society. How should we deal with it?
9. What is the role of parent–teacher organizations?
10. As a principal, you will be involved in the hiring of staff. What specific qualities would you be looking for in candidates?
11. As principal, how would you strike a balance between being the instructional leader of the school and managing the day-to-day operations of the building?
12. From your perspective, what are the key elements of the teacher evaluation process?
13. What suggestions do you have in meeting the needs of the marginal teacher?
14. At what point does the principal need to say no to the parents of a special needs child who are persistent and will not take no for an answer?
15. Explain how you might handle a situation in which you know the teacher has erred and the parent is adamant about taking action against the teacher.
16. Please tell us about a confrontation you have had with a parent or staff member—how you handled it and the outcome.
17. Explain how you would design and implement a behavior plan for a student who is regularly experiencing discipline problems.
18. A new leader usually means some degree of change. In addition to explaining how you view and handle change in general, please tell us of a change initiative and/or educational innovation that you facilitated in your professional career.
19. Please talk about teacher accountability as related to classroom performance.
20. What are your beliefs concerning homework?
21. What are some ways you would work with staff to create and sustain a variety of opportunities for parent and community involvement in the life of the school?
22. How would you create a schedule to accomplish all that is expected in a school day?

CHAPTER 21

23. When a normally diligent custodian leaves you a note saying that he refuses to clean a certain classroom because the teacher and his or her students leave it such a mess each day, how would you respond?

24. Describe your involvement with the nonteaching staff in an elementary school.

25. On occasion, a principal makes a decision to take a certain course of action but is prevented from doing so by the superintendent. Have you had any such experience, and, if so, how did you deal with the rejection? If not, how would you anticipate dealing with such a circumstance?

NOTES

INTERVIEW NOTES FOR PRINCIPAL OF MIDDLE SCHOOL

Interview Date   Candidate(s) Interviewed   Questions Used

Notes/Additional Questions

PRINCIPAL OF MIDDLE SCHOOL

1. Please imagine that we are a group of parents attending a PTA meeting, and explain to us your concept of the middle school.
2. What are the professional journals telling us about the middle school of the future?
3. How do goals become an integral part of the school, and what are some indicators that would tell you this?
4. As a principal, what will be the role of the assistant principal(s) in your building?
5. We live in troubled times. What measures must be in place for our students to be safe in school?
6. What experience have you had in developing a building budget, and how would you approach the task as a principal?
7. Please tell us about a confrontation you have had with a parent or a staff member—how you handled it and the outcome.
8. Our building will soon undergo a major renovation. What are some of the issues that would need to be addressed to keep the building running smoothly during the course of these renovations?
9. Please describe how you would go about working with a veteran teacher whom you determine is ineffective.
10. Everybody has experienced successful tricks of the trade, things that really worked for him or her, that they bring from position to position. Share one or two of these that you would share with our school if appointed.
11. Please discuss curriculum development as well as the use of technology in today's middle school.
12. Please discuss differentiated instruction.
13. Please discuss special education inclusion.
14. Please discuss alternative education.
15. A new leader usually means some degree of change. In addition to explaining how you view and handle change in general, please tell us of a change initiative and/or educational innovation that you facilitated in your professional career.
16. Relative to change, how, if at all, would you revise the process?
17. Teachers are challenged, and at times frustrated, by the need to cover a certain amount of instructional material each year *and* provide in-depth instruction. How can these two needs be reconciled within an instructional program?
18. Please talk about teacher accountability as related to classroom performance?
19. What will be your role in the evaluation of teachers if you are the principal?
20. You were sent a copy of the current middle school student handbook and asked to come prepared to comment on the document. Please share these remarks with us at this time.
21. As a principal, would you view the rules and consequences in a student handbook as a guideline or as being cast in stone?
22. What are your beliefs concerning homework?
23. Should the school district set homework requirements for all teachers to follow?
24. If we were to visit your school and speak with members of your staff, how would they describe your availability as well as your visibility?
25. In addition to what takes place in the classroom, students are involved in a number of school-related activities. What is their importance, and how do these activities fit into the total school program?

INTERVIEW NOTES FOR PRINCIPAL OF HIGH SCHOOL

Interview Date   Candidate(s) Interviewed   Questions Used

Notes/Additional Questions

PRINCIPAL OF HIGH SCHOOL

1. Please summarize your professional experiences, and highlight those you feel have best prepared you for a position as a principal.
2. Please describe your leadership style and your basic approach to communicating with students, staff, and parents.
3. Please give us an example of how you have delegated duties to others.
4. How would you react if, after delegating responsibilities, you discovered halfway through the project that no progress was being made?
5. Is it proper to delegate responsibilities and, at the same time, dictate what the outcome should be?
6. What would be the role of your assistant principal(s)?
7. What personal and professional qualities would you expect of your assistant principal(s)?
8. What social level would you maintain between yourself and staff?
9. How would you communicate with the student body?
10. Other than attending ball games and being in the cafeteria, what are some unique and different ways you could be visible to the student body?
11. What percentage of students in your present school are you able to call by their first name?
12. What is the role of the student council?
13. Should there be censorship of the school newspaper and yearbook?
14. What immediate steps would you take if a student demonstration were to occur in your school?
15. What are your views on student fund-raising?
16. How would you communicate with parents?
17. What is the role of parent organizations?
18. Can you give us an example of how parent organizations may have to be restricted?
19. How do we convince more parents to be active in our schools?
20. How do you deal with the parent who ignores a request to attend a conference with a teacher or the principal?
21. How do you deal with the parent who becomes obnoxious or out of control at a conference?
22. How do you honor those parents who contribute to the school?
23. Should parents have a role in the hiring of teachers?
24. Should parents work in the same school their children attend?
25. How would you utilize parent volunteers?
26. Please talk about teacher accountability.
27. What makes a good teacher?
28. How would you assign teacher duties?
29. How often would you schedule teacher meetings?
30. What is the role and function of teacher meetings?

CHAPTER 23

31. You were sent a copy of the current student handbook and asked to come prepared to comment on the document. Please share your comments with us at this time.

32. Please explain how you would design and implement a behavioral modification plan for a student who is regularly experiencing discipline problems.

33. Please tell us your philosophy concerning student disciplinary detention.

34. When detentions do not work, what is the next step?

35. When everything you have tried does not change inappropriate student behavior, what comes next?

36. A teacher demands that a student be permanently removed from his class. How do you deal with this?

37. Please describe your approach to handling disciplinary matters.

38. Describe how you would go about working with a veteran teacher whom you determine is ineffective?

39. What beliefs and skills do you bring to ensure the advancement of technology in the education of our students?

40. What is your level of computer expertise?

41. Where would you want to see computers used in your high school?

42. What measures would you put in place to prevent computers from being used for inappropriate functions?

43. Should all teachers have proficient computer capability?

44. Technology is expensive. How would you handle the financial aspect?

45. Other than computers, what other aspects of technology should the district be concerned with at the high school level?

46. What experience have you had in developing budgets?

47. How do you develop a school budget?

48. How do you go about making cuts in proposed budgets?

49. Which line items in your school budget would not be considered for cuts?

50. What experience have you had in developing student schedules?

51. What is your opinion of block scheduling?

52. Including both your teaching and administrative experience, what kinds of schedules do you have experience with and which do you prefer?

53. How do you schedule time for everything?

54. What are some critical factors that must be considered in building a student schedule?

55. What is the role of student activities and athletics?

56. Please discuss eligibility concerning student activities and athletics.

57. How would you react to allegations of student hazing in athletics?

58. Please discuss your philosophy concerning student organizations taking overnight trips.

59. Let us give you a hypothetical situation: A student has an average just below the cutoff grade in one subject that is keeping him from playing a varsity sport. His furious parents are in your office and accuse the teacher of not liking their son and of being unfair, stating that they are taxpayers and will go to the board of education. The teacher has told you that this student needs to do the work and will not yield on the grade. The coach is not happy with the teacher and has stressed the student's importance to the team. The student lives for athletics, and that factor is keeping this student enrolled in school. What steps would you take to resolve this situation?

60. How many after-school activities, such as ball games and concerts, can a principal realistically attend?

NOTES

INTERVIEW NOTES FOR ASSISTANT PRINCIPAL

Interview Date   Candidate(s) Interviewed   Questions Used

Notes/Additional Questions

ASSISTANT PRINCIPAL

1. Do you aspire to be a principal?
2. Teachers expect assistant principals to deal with student discipline. Please describe your approach to handling disciplinary matters.
3. Please explain how you would design and implement a behavioral modification plan for a student who is regularly experiencing discipline problems.
4. Please share with us your philosophy concerning student discipline.
5. How would you administer discipline as an assistant principal?
6. Please describe a typical day in the life of an assistant principal.
7. What do you see as the role of the special education teacher in the mainstream classroom?
8. Describe how you would go about working with a veteran teacher whom you determine is ineffective.
9. What experience have you had in developing budgets and student schedules?
10. We live in troubled times. What measures must be in place for our students to be safe in school?
11. What beliefs and skills do you bring to ensure the advancement of technology in the education of our students?
12. Budgets are limited. With that in mind, how would you prioritize spending to enhance the use of technology in our schools?
13. How would you work to develop the acceptance of diversity for all members of the school community?
14. How do your perceive your role in working with guidance, special education, and other support services staff in meeting the needs of all students?
15. From your readings in professional journals, please discuss curriculum development in today's [*elementary/middle/high*] school and how you see yourself in that process.
16. In addition to what takes place in the classroom, students are very involved in a number of school-related activities. What is their importance, and how do these activities fit into the total school program?
17. Please give us your views on cutting students from clubs and athletic teams at the middle school level.
18. What are some ways you would work with staff to create and sustain a variety of opportunities for parent and community involvement in the life of the school?
19. How would you utilize parent volunteers?
20. Please give us an example of something you did, or that you were involved in, that would demonstrate your leadership style.
21. What do you expect to observe when entering the school's library?
22. Place yourself in the role of a middle school assistant principal who is meeting with a newly hired paraprofessional, with no experience, on her first day of work. What do you want this person to know about the middle school student, and what advice would you give?

CHAPTER 24

23. Putting aside what your current school does or what you know about our school district, how do you personally believe the use of technology can be improved in our schools, and what kind of faculty training would this require?
24. We are interested in your beliefs concerning heterogeneous grouping, students with special needs, and inclusion. How do we ensure that the instructional needs of *all* of our students are being met within the context of heterogeneous grouping?
25. What do you think is missing in today's [*elementary/middle/high*] schools?

NOTES

INTERVIEW NOTES FOR DEPARTMENT HEAD

Interview Date   Candidate(s) Interviewed   Questions Used

Notes/Additional Questions

25

DEPARTMENT HEAD

1. Although the committee has had an opportunity to examine your résumé, please take a moment to tell us about the qualifications you have that specifically relate to your candidacy for the position of department head.
2. As you visit classrooms and observe members of your staff, what teaching standards are important to you, and what will you do should you discover a teacher not achieving those standards?
3. Please give us an example of how you have directly assisted a marginal teacher.
4. How will you organize and run department meetings?
5. What is your philosophy concerning the necessity of department meetings?
6. In which areas are you able to conduct in-service workshops?
7. What qualities will you look for when hiring teachers?
8. When looking at a teacher candidate's résumé, how much weight should be given to knowledge of the subject area as opposed to the teacher's effectiveness?
9. This position requires supervision of two separate departments. How must you manage your time to be fair to both?
10. Because you will be supervising two departments, do you have thoughts, either pro or con, as to how these two departments could work together?
11. What are the minimum expectations this system should have relative to the use of technology in this department?
12. How have you used technology in your past positions?
13. What minimum standards would you expect from your department staff?
14. What percentage of the department budget would you appropriate to technology?
15. What is your experience in developing budgets?
16. How can we reduce the budget in the area of textbooks?
17. What do the national journals tell us is the best approach for teaching [*insert discipline*] today and beyond, and do you agree?
18. How do you view the role of a department head as related to the principal?
19. If you and the building principal have a disagreement that cannot be solved between the two of you, how would you remedy the situation?
20. How would you handle a student complaint that a teacher is not effective in the classroom?

INTERVIEW NOTES FOR ATHLETIC DIRECTOR

Interview Date   Candidate(s) Interviewed   Questions Used

Notes/Additional Questions

26

ATHLETIC DIRECTOR

1. What do you consider the role of the athletic director to be?
2. Can you envision circumstances where the athletic director would have to step in and overrule the mandate of a coach?
3. What qualities do you look for when hiring coaches?
4. You have a choice of two equally qualified coaches for a high school position. One teaches in the high school and one in the middle school. Would their teaching assignment influence your choice and why?
5. Talk to us about hiring an individual to coach a team of the opposite sex?
6. Would you be willing to hire coaches who are not on the teaching staff?
7. What will you do to satisfy parents that coaches are well trained and qualified?
8. How would you respond if a coach were to ask you to intercede with a teacher concerning a student's grade?
9. Talk to us about Title IX and how you interpret that legislation.
10. How do you work with a parent who makes allegations that his or her son is being discriminated against by the coach in such areas as playing time?
11. How do you respond to a parent's allegations that students in a certain sport are being driven beyond expectations and becoming ill?
12. How do you respond to the criticism of weight loss in certain sports?
13. What is your position on adopting a uniform procedure or policy for our coaching staff to use when addressing the use of nutritional supplements by student athletes?
14. What would you do if you learned that a coach is advocating the use of steroids?
15. Should high school athletes undergo drug testing?
16. Talk to us about the relationship of practice sessions to the rest of the student's responsibilities at home or at work.
17. Should athletic teams practice on Saturday and Sunday?
18. What would you tell your coaches relative to cutting members from a team?
19. The high school band director is not in favor of marching bands and having to organize the entire fall schedule to accommodate the football program. You disagree. What steps would you take to resolve the matter?
20. How much of the athletic program should be financed through fund-raising?
21. Have you developed athletic budgets?
22. If the athletic budget had to be cut, would you consider the sports that require large expenditures more than sports that do not in proposing cuts?
23. What guidelines would you establish for college recruiters?
24. At what point do you replace a losing coach?
25. Should high schools replace a losing coach?

INTERVIEW NOTES FOR TEACHER: PRESCHOOL

Interview Date   Candidate(s) Interviewed   Questions Used

Notes/Additional Questions

27

TEACHER: PRESCHOOL

1. What is the extent of your experience with preschool programs?
2. What constitutes a properly developed birth-to-three program?
3. What do you consider to be the strengths and weaknesses of the Head Start program?
4. Please describe a visit you have made to a student's home to discuss the preschool child and how you assessed the total experience both from the parents' reaction and from your expectations.
5. How should a town evaluate the need for early childhood programs?
6. How will early childhood programs develop in the next five to ten years?
7. Please talk about the classroom environment necessary for early childhood programs.
8. What elements are necessary for an early childhood program to succeed?
9. How would you structure the early childhood curriculum?
10. What differences would be evident in an early childhood classroom as opposed to a kindergarten classroom?
11. How would you organize your classroom management for preschool children?
12. Please take us through the daily routine of a preschool classroom.
13. Please give us an example of a typical problem a teacher might encounter with a preschool child and how you would approach the parents to notify them of this problem.
14. Please describe the system that you would use in lesson planning that would ensure that you are guiding learning through a continuum of related skills of the preschool child.
15. Please describe the system you would use for preschool child assessment.

INTERVIEW NOTES FOR TEACHER: GRADES K-6

Interview Date   Candidate(s) Interviewed   Questions Used

Notes/Additional Questions

28

TEACHER: GRADES K–6

1. How do you determine the role of academic versus social time in the kindergarten?
2. Please give us examples of literature appropriate for kindergarten.
3. What advice do you give parents who, because of the birth date, are thinking of waiting one year before enrolling the child for kindergarten?
4. How would you use technology in the kindergarten classroom?
5. Have you worked with children from a Head Start or other early childhood program, and has that made a difference?
6. Describe early adolescent learners and how they learn.
7. What experience have you had in differentiating classroom instruction?
8. What experience do you have with looping?
9. What experience do you have with teaching combined grades?
10. What are the pros and cons of teaching a combined grade classroom?
11. Please discuss reading support programs for at-risk students in the primary grades.
12. Describe what we would see if we walked into your primary-level classroom.
13. How would you get all of the children actively involved?
14. How do you determine when a lesson is best handled through individual, group, or whole-class teaching?
15. What steps do you take to assess a child's knowledge when the student arrives well into the school year?
16. Please discuss inclusion and how that impacts your classroom.
17. Please discuss the teaching of mathematics at the elementary level.
18. Which reading series are you familiar with, and which do you prefer?
19. How would you deal with a reading consultant if you had reservations about the approach being used in your classroom?
20. Please give us the titles of some excellent children's books.
21. Would you use learning centers, and, if so, how would you organize these?
22. Please talk about the use of technology in your classroom.
23. Please tell us about a successful thematic unit you have used.
24. A parent expresses concern that her child is not being treated well by the other children and offers to speak to your class about their family cultural heritage so that this treatment will improve. How would you respond?
25. Please describe any curriculum materials you have developed.
26. Would you prefer to teach the slow or advanced learner?
27. The PTA gives you $500 for your classroom. How do you use it?
28. What do you hope to accomplish on the first day of school?
29. What steps would you take for a child with difficulty grasping group concepts?
30. How would you meet the needs of the superior child?

INTERVIEW NOTES FOR TEACHER: ENGLISH 7–12

Interview Date   Candidate(s) Interviewed   Questions Used

Notes/Additional Questions

29

TEACHER: ENGLISH 7–12

1. Which English department subjects are you most comfortable teaching?
2. Do the typical English offerings in today's high schools meet the needs of our students?
3. Who is your favorite author and why?
4. Please give us the title of two books that you have found to be most successful with middle school students.
5. Please give us your recommendation of four books that every high school student should be required to read prior to graduation.
6. If you were provided with funds to subscribe to three periodicals for use in your classroom, which ones would you select?
7. If your English class is composed of students with various levels of academic achievement, how do you plan your lessons when assigning a novel to read?
8. Please give us an outline of your course of study if you were teaching a high school course in British literature.
9. What reading would you assign to coordinate with a social studies unit on the Civil War at the middle school level?
10. How would you introduce a unit on poetry to middle school students?
11. How can we improve our students' use of grammar?
12. Do you use diagramming when teaching parts of speech?
13. How would you teach the writing process in grade [*insert grade*]?
14. Do you have any teaching experience in media, speech, or drama?
15. What impact has the computer and word processing software had on the work of today's students?

INTERVIEW NOTES FOR TEACHER: MATH 7–12

Interview Date   Candidate(s) Interviewed   Questions Used

Notes/Additional Questions

TEACHER: MATH 7–12

1. Which subjects are you most comfortable teaching?
2. Which subjects would you not select to teach and why?
3. What do you personally think of the math offerings in today's high schools?
4. What suggestions do you have for a district whose standardized mathematics test scores are below the state average?
5. Why do you believe school districts have students who score below the state average on standardized mathematics examinations?
6. If you were invited to address a PTA meeting on standardized mathematics testing, what points, both pro and con, would you cover?
7. Are you familiar with methods of teaching mathematics to students in elementary schools, and, if so, what is your opinion on how this is accomplished?
8. At which grade should algebra be introduced?
9. Do you find today's students prepared for the mathematics offerings in our secondary schools?
10. What is your opinion of the student use of calculators?
11. Do you favor the use of calculators on examinations?
12. How do you answer the criticism that, if it were not for cash registers that tell us how much change we should receive, high school graduates would have no idea of how to make change?
13. How has the computer changed your approach to the teaching of mathematics?
14. Have you ever worked with students in a course such as SAT preparation?
15. How can we better prepare our students for the SATs?

INTERVIEW NOTES FOR TEACHER: SCIENCE 7-12

Interview Date   Candidate(s) Interviewed   Questions Used

Notes/Additional Questions

31

TEACHER: SCIENCE 7–12

1. One of your chemistry students complains that there is too much math in your course and that he is "terrible in math." The in-class instruction has not worked with him, and the student seeks extra help. What strategies might you employ in a one-on-one help session to help him gain confidence?
2. What steps can be taken to improve science offerings for the low- to middle-achieving students?
3. If a student or parent objects to dissection in your biology [*or anatomy and physiology*] class, what do you say or do?
4. How do you react to the complaint that we continue to include dissection in our classrooms when a computer program can accomplish the same task?
5. During a discussion of evolutionary theory, a student insists that creation accounts for the diversity of life. How do you address this person's objections to your approach?
6. A student refuses to wear required goggles for a lab during which she will be handling acids and bases. Other than direct punishment, how can you convince the student to wear the goggles?
7. Please tell us about an experience you have had with a student who caused an accident in a laboratory experiment and how you handled the situation.
8. Describe how you would organize a lesson to emphasize safety in the laboratory.
9. What are your minimum expectations in the areas of the physical facility and classroom equipment in order for you to teach science properly to today's high school students?
10. How do you use the computer as part of today's science curriculum?
11. Have you worked with any particular scheduling programs for both classes and labs that improve the teaching of science?
12. Which sciences are you certified to teach?
13. Which subjects are you most comfortable teaching?
14. Which subjects would you not select to teach and why?
15. What do you personally think of the science offerings in today's high schools?

INTERVIEW NOTES FOR TEACHER: HISTORY/SOCIAL STUDIES 7–12

Interview Date   Candidate(s) Interviewed   Questions Used

Notes/Additional Questions

32

TEACHER: HISTORY/SOCIAL STUDIES 7–12

1. Which history/social studies subjects are you most comfortable teaching?
2. What do you personally think of social studies offerings in today's high schools?
3. As a history/social studies teacher, how do you plan to "change the world"?
4. How can your teaching of history make the student a better citizen in later life?
5. To what extent do you envision interdisciplinary learning as part of a social studies curriculum?
6. What methodologies of social studies teaching would you employ?
7. If you were teaching a course in U.S. history, what percentage of time would be spent on each era?
8. Whatever happened to the teaching of geography?
9. Which specific events in the history of the United States within the past ten years do you find have evoked student interest and why?
10. Under an ideal curriculum, create a 9–12 social studies scope and sequence, and explain why you chose the scope and sequence you did.
11. Using the State of (*insert state*) Social Studies Competencies, which do you believe are most important for a student to learn before graduating from high school?
12. How much dependence do you give to the use of audiovisual aids in your teaching?
13. Are there any television programs you might recommend as part of a history/social studies unit of study?
14. If the topic of protests were to surface in your classroom and you sensed that some students were planning to organize such a movement, how would you handle the situation, and what advice would you give?
15. Please discuss the impact 9/11 has had on your teaching approach.

INTERVIEW NOTES FOR TEACHER: FOREIGN LANGUAGES

Interview Date   Candidate(s) Interviewed   Questions Used

Notes/Additional Questions

33

TEACHER: FOREIGN LANGUAGES

1. Which languages are you certified to teach?
2. Which languages are you most comfortable teaching?
3. Which languages would you not select to teach and why?
4. What do you personally think of the foreign language offerings in today's high schools?
5. Please discuss the value of Latin in today's foreign language department offerings.
6. At which grade should the study of foreign languages begin?
7. What approach would you use for teaching foreign languages in the elementary schools?
8. Which language(s) would you recommend for study at the elementary level and why?
9. What advice do you give to students and parents when there is a question as to which foreign language to study?
10. How do you respond to students who express interest in a particular language because it is "easier"?
11. What expectations should we expect for a student completing one year of study of a foreign language?
12. Please give us an overview of how you begin instruction in (*insert language*) and what is covered in the first two months.
13. How would you use technology in your foreign language classroom?
14. How and when do you introduce the study of the culture of the language being studied in your classroom?
15. What is your opinion of the importance of overseas field trips that are often taken by foreign language classes?

INTERVIEW NOTES FOR TEACHER: BUSINESS EDUCATION

Interview Date   Candidate(s) Interviewed   Questions Used

Notes/Additional Questions

34

TEACHER: BUSINESS EDUCATION

1. The business education offerings have changed dramatically over the past years. How will this department change even further in the next five years?
2. How will future changes in the department impact budget allocations?
3. Please tell us about your keyboarding skills.
4. Which software programs are you able to teach?
5. Which software programs do you favor using for the teaching of keyboarding skills to students in grades 7 through 12?
6. What advice would you give relative to the teaching of keyboarding in the elementary grades to better prepare students for the offerings in your department?
7. With all of the choices available, which software programs best prepare students for their future education or employment opportunities?
8. What training do you have to enable you to teach accounting courses?
9. Take us through a beginning accounting course, and tell us what the expected outcome would be for the first year.
10. Do you have experience in teaching retail merchandising and/or marketing?
11. What hands-on experiences would you design for students in your retail merchandising and/or marketing course?
12. Please tell us about a student-designed hands-on marketing application that was successful in one of your former classes.
13. How do you approach the teaching of research in a retail merchandising and/or marketing course?
14. How would you approach the teaching of macro- and microeconomics?
15. Is there a specific textbook you prefer using to teach economics at the high school level?

INTERVIEW NOTES FOR TEACHER: MUSIC/GENERAL MUSIC K-6 AND CHORUS

Interview Date   Candidate(s) Interviewed   Questions Used

Notes/Additional Questions

TEACHER: MUSIC/GENERAL MUSIC K–6 AND CHORUS

1. What is your applied performance area?
2. What is your public performance background in your applied area?
3. What are your keyboard skills?
4. What are your keyboard sight-reading skills?
5. What are your keyboard transposition skills?
6. What are your conducting skills?
7. Do you play guitar well enough to use in a classroom?
8. Which instruments can you comfortably demonstrate in the classroom?
9. Why do schools teach general music to elementary children?
10. How often do you recommend elementary students receive general music instruction for the curriculum to be covered?
11. Is it important for the elementary classroom teacher to know what you taught in your lesson on a particular day?
12. What is your background in Kodaly, Orff, and Dalcrose?
13. Do you believe in programs such as Kodaly, Orff, and Dalcrose?
14. Would you use a textbook in your general music classes?
15. Is there a textbook series you are familiar with that you would recommend?
16. Must you purchase the coordinated recordings and charts available from the publisher for the textbook to be effective?
17. Are these textbooks worth the cost?
18. If given an amount of money, would you purchase textbooks or equipment?
19. Describe a musical game you could use in a [*select a grade level*] grade classroom.
20. If you were to do a unit on [*select a historical period—e.g., classical, contemporary*] with a grade [*select a grade level*] class, which composer(s) would you select?
21. The entire [*select a grade level*] grade is doing a unit on [*select a topic—e.g., space, Native Americans*]. Please give us an example of how you would plan your music lessons to fit this project.
22. We don't have a music room, and you will have to move from room to room with a cart. How do you manage this task?
23. The budget does not permit the purchase of a [*select a piece of equipment—e.g., piano, stereo*]. How will you work around this constraint?
24. Have you had experience in teaching general music to special education classes?
25. What kind of field trip would be appropriate for a grade [*select a grade level*] general music class?
26. What advice would you give to the principal or PTA wishing to sponsor a professional music ensemble for a school assembly program?
27. Would you teach [*select a popular type of music—e.g., rock and roll, rap*] as part of the general music class? Why or why not?
28. How would you organize an elementary school chorus?

CHAPTER 35

29. Would you audition for chorus membership?

30. Should any student be turned away from chorus participation?

31. How would you recruit boys for the chorus?

32. How often should the chorus perform in public?

33. What kind of literature would you select?

34. How would you program music for a Christmas concert?

35. Would you conduct the chorus or conduct from the keyboard?

36. Would you use prepared tapes to accompany the chorus?

37. How would you select chorus soloists?

38. How much part singing can we expect to hear from an elementary school chorus?

39. Would you want your chorus to attend adjudication or competitive festivals?

40. How would you interact with the band/orchestra director?

NOTES

INTERVIEW NOTES FOR TEACHER: MUSIC/SECONDARY INSTRUMENTAL WITH PERFORMING GROUPS

Interview Date   Candidate(s) Interviewed   Questions Used

Notes/Additional Questions

36

TEACHER: MUSIC/SECONDARY INSTRUMENTAL WITH PERFORMING GROUPS

1. What is your applied performance area?
2. What is your public performance background in your applied area?
3. What are your keyboard skills?
4. What are your keyboard sight-reading skills?
5. What are your keyboard transposition skills?
6. What are your conducting skills?
7. Which instruments can you perform on adequately enough for demonstration purposes?
8. Which instruments do you feel inadequate in teaching?
9. Is your strength in woodwinds, brass, percussion, or strings?
10. At what age should we begin instrumental instruction?
11. Do physical attributes dictate the choice of instrument to be studied?
12. How do you plan for instrument balance within a musical organization?
13. Which instruments, if any, should the school system provide and why?
14. How would we budget for necessary instruments?
15. Should schools provide a better-quality instrument for advanced high school players?
16. Some instruments require expensive accessories such as oboe reeds. Who should pay for these?
17. How do you deal with the student who will not practice?
18. What kind of literature should we expect a middle school band/orchestra to perform?
19. What kind of literature should we expect a high school band/orchestra to perform?
20. Please cite five specific compositions that students should be exposed to before graduating from the high school band/orchestra program.
21. How do you teach intonation?
22. Would you provide opportunities for ensemble work?
23. How would you fit ensemble experience into your program?
24. Very few of our students study privately outside school. How do those students who do not study privately learn?
25. How should lessons be organized for instrumental students?
26. Would students who study through the school's lesson program learn from method books or band/orchestra literature?
27. Describe the proper embouchure for a [*select an instrument*].
28. How do you grade instrumental music students?
29. A student wants to drop band/orchestra because the grade she is receiving is lowering her overall average and class rank. How do you respond?
30. What is your philosophy of marching band programs?
31. How would you organize a marching band program?

CHAPTER 36

32. Should marching band be part of the academic band program?

33. Should marching band be required of all band students?

34. If marching is a program requirement, how do you accommodate the student who works and cannot participate on weekends?

35. Would your marching band be part of a competitive program?

36. What kind of field trips would you plan for the band/orchestra?

37. How would such field trips be financed?

38. What is the role of jazz ensembles in the school music program?

39. How do you provide a performing experience for the numerous guitar players and drummers in our school?

40. Can jazz improvisation be taught?

NOTES

INTERVIEW NOTES FOR TEACHER: MUSIC/SECONDARY VOCAL WITH PERFORMING GROUPS

Interview Date   Candidate(s) Interviewed   Questions Used

Notes/Additional Questions

TEACHER: MUSIC/SECONDARY VOCAL WITH PERFORMING GROUPS

1. What is your applied performance area?
2. What is your public performance background in your applied area?
3. What are your keyboard skills?
4. What are your keyboard sight-reading skills?
5. What are your keyboard transposition skills?
6. What are your conducting skills?
7. How would you organize the chorus program at the middle/high school?
8. Would choral groups be open to all those interested?
9. How would you recruit singers?
10. How would you recruit boys into the chorus?
11. How would you organize a high school chorus?
12. Would you audition for chorus membership?
13. Should any student be turned away from chorus participation?
14. How often should the chorus perform in public?
15. What kind of literature would you select?
16. How would you program music for a Christmas concert?
17. Would you conduct the chorus or conduct from the keyboard?
18. Would you use prepared tapes to accompany the chorus?
19. Assuming a well-balanced chorus and a proficient pianist, please cite five specific compositions that students should be exposed to before graduating from a high school choral program.
20. How would you approach teaching a spiritual to your chorus?
21. How do you respond to a complaint that the chorus is performing a purely religious work such as the Beethoven *Mass in C Major*?
22. How would you select chorus soloists?
23. Where do you place the boy with an unchanged voice?
24. Would you use girls to fill in the tenor parts?
25. How many boys need to enroll to move from soprano, alto, bass (SAB) to soprano, alto, tenor, bass (SATB) literature?
26. Would you use student accompanists?
27. What level of part singing can we expect from a high school chorus?
28. What kind of field trips would you plan for your chorus?
29. Would you want your chorus to attend adjudication or competitive festivals?
30. How would you interact with the band/orchestra director?
31. Instrumental students receive lessons. Should this also hold true for choral students?

CHAPTER 37

32. How do you grade choral music students?
33. A student wants to drop chorus because the grade he is receiving is lowering his overall average and class rank. How do you respond?
34. Should chorus be a club or a graded music course?
35. What kind of garment would your choral performing groups wear for performances?
36. Considering the price of music, why not make photocopies?
37. What is your philosophy concerning jazz choirs?
38. What is your philosophy concerning show choirs?
39. Should jazz and show choirs be part of the academic music program?
40. How do we finance programs such as jazz and show choirs?

NOTES

INTERVIEW NOTES FOR TEACHER: ART K-8

Interview Date   Candidate(s) Interviewed   Questions Used

Notes/Additional Questions

TEACHER: ART K–8

1. Please talk about your professional work as an artist.
2. Have you exhibited professionally?
3. Have you sold any of your works?
4. How would you organize your classes to accommodate individual achievement levels?
5. How would you provide a quality lesson if required to push a cart of supplies from room to room?
6. Are you familiar with discipline-based art education (DBAE)?
7. What guidance would you give to a student with excellent art skills?
8. Please talk about teaching drawing.
9. Would you incorporate poster contests as part of your curriculum?
10. Should poster contests be part of an art program?
11. Please talk about teaching perspective in grade [*insert grade*].
12. What would your reaction be to teaching photography at the elementary level?
13. Does the teaching of crafts have a role in an elementary school art program?
14. Of all the crafts, which would you select to teach and why?
15. Where does the teaching of art history fit into the elementary art program?
16. Which movement in art are you most comfortable teaching?
17. Which museums near our districts might you take students to on a field trip?
18. Other than museums, where else would you take art students on a field trip?
19. How could the art department make contributions to the entire school?
20. Should the art department be expected to assist in such things as stage production scenery, dance decorations, and bulletin boards?
21. Have you ever developed a budget for an elementary school art program?
22. If students were expected to provide materials due to a limited budget, which items would you suggest?
23. Why should or shouldn't students be expected to provide art materials?
24. Give us examples of how you would exhibit student art.
25. Let us assume the entire grade [*insert grade level*] will be doing a unit on [*insert topic*]. How would you plan your art lessons for that grade during this unit?
26. Please talk about art clubs as an extracurricular activity.
27. Please discuss how you grade art students.
28. Is it possible for the student who is, as commonly referred to, "not good at art" to receive an A?
29. How would you react to the parent who approaches you requesting that you provide private instruction in art for his or her child?
30. Please give us examples of how the computer can be used in the teaching of art.

INTERVIEW NOTES FOR TEACHER: ART 9-12

Interview Date   Candidate(s) Interviewed   Questions Used

Notes/Additional Questions

39

TEACHER: ART 9–12

1. Tell me about your professional work as an artist.
2. Have you exhibited professionally?
3. Have you sold any of your works?
4. What courses should a high school with [*insert number*] art teachers offer?
5. How would you organize your classes to accommodate individual achievement levels?
6. Are you familiar with discipline-based art education (known as DBAE)?
7. Should you find a freshman with excellent art skills, how do you approach him or her to begin a serious study of art?
8. Would you encourage a gifted student to pursue art as a career?
9. How would you work with a student who is interested in a career in art?
10. Please talk about teaching drawing.
11. Please talk about teaching oils.
12. Please talk about teaching watercolors.
13. Please talk about teaching perspective.
14. Can you teach photography?
15. Please talk about teaching photography.
16. Please talk about teaching sculpture.
17. Does the teaching of crafts have a role in public school art programs?
18. If the curriculum required you to teach one of the following four crafts—ceramics, stained glass, macramé, or jewelry—which would you select and why?
19. Where and how does the teaching of art history fit into the art program?
20. Which movement in art (i.e., Impressionism, Baroque, etc.) are you most comfortable teaching?
21. Which museums near our districts might you take students on a field trip?
22. Other than museums, where else would you take art students on a field trip?
23. Should poster contests be part of an art program?
24. How could the art department make contributions to the entire school?
25. Should the art department be expected to assist in such things as stage production scenery, dance decorations, and bulletin boards?
26. Have you ever developed a budget for a high school art program?
27. If students were expected to provide materials due to a limited budget, which items would you suggest?
28. How would you react to the parent who approaches you requesting that you provide private instruction in art for his or her child?
29. Give us examples of how you would exhibit student art.
30. Please give us examples of how the computer can be used in the teaching of art.

INTERVIEW NOTES FOR TEACHER: PHYSICAL EDUCATION K–8

Interview Date   Candidate(s) Interviewed   Questions Used

Notes/Additional Questions

40

TEACHER: PHYSICAL EDUCATION K–8

1. How often would you recommend students participate in a physical education class at the elementary school level?
2. What kinds of learning experiences can you provide children in elementary school in order for them to be physically competent?
3. Please give us three examples of an activity you would use with grade [*insert grade level*] students.
4. Please give us an example of an activity that is used in most grades and what your expectations are from that activity as the student progresses in age.
5. Would you address elementary student weight problems as part of your program?
6. In what ways could you incorporate reading into the daily physical education curriculum?
7. Does competition belong in the elementary physical education curriculum?
8. How should the physical education curriculum at the elementary level coordinate with, or prepare students for, the secondary program?
9. Is there a way to provide for individual interests, as opposed to team participation, with elementary physical education classes? If so, how would you go about accomplishing that?
10. What are your views on adventure-based programming in physical education?
11. How do you grade students in physical education?
12. Is it possible for a student who is not athletic to achieve an A in physical education?
13. How would you deal with a parent who is concerned that his or her child does not want to come to school on days that physical education is scheduled?
14. A teacher brings his class to physical education and picks them up at the end of your class. In many cases, the teacher does not know what is happening in your class but also may not care. How would you deal with this situation?
15. Should your department have any interaction with youth athletic leagues?

INTERVIEW NOTES FOR TEACHER: PHYSICAL EDUCATION AND HEALTH 9-12

Interview Date   Candidate(s) Interviewed   Questions Used

Notes/Additional Questions

41

TEACHER: PHYSICAL EDUCATION AND HEALTH 9–12

1. How often would you recommend students participate in a physical education class?
2. How many students should be scheduled for a physical education class?
3. Should physical education classes be coed?
4. Why have physical education programs done away with required uniforms, and is that issue at all important?
5. How do you deal with the student who is reluctant to participate in physical education class?
6. How do you deal with the student who is uncomfortable in a locker room atmosphere?
7. Please tell us about the kinds of activities you organize for both indoor and outdoor classes.
8. How often do you hold a lecture-style physical education class, and what topics would you cover in such a class setting?
9. Please discuss the concepts of team sports versus individual activities that provide athletic experiences and exercise in the physical education classroom.
10. Are there any activities that you would require of all students in a physical education class?
11. Should students who participate in varsity or junior varsity athletics be required to take physical education during that sport's season?
12. What is your reaction to offering a dance program to meet the physical education requirement?
13. Please talk about equipment requirements for today's physical education programs.
14. How do you grade students in physical education?
15. Is it possible for a student who is not athletic to achieve an A in physical education?
16. Please discuss the approach you would use to teach health education.
17. Please give us an example of how you have dealt with a parent who has concerns about a topic being covered in a health education class.
18. How do you deal with the student who is embarrassed in a health education class and insists on leaving or not attending?
19. Is there any topic in a health education class that you feel uncomfortable teaching?
20. Are there any topics that are not included in the health education curriculum that should be included?

INTERVIEW NOTES FOR TEACHER: VOCATIONAL EDUCATION

Interview Date   Candidate(s) Interviewed   Questions Used

Notes/Additional Questions

42

TEACHER: VOCATIONAL EDUCATION

1. Please talk to us about how you would incorporate technology education curriculum offerings in today's middle/high school.
2. When you perused our course offerings, what pros and cons did you discover?
3. Which students enroll for courses in your department, and how would you promote your department to increase enrollments?
4. Which courses do you feel most comfortable teaching?
5. Please tell us about your desktop publishing skills.
6. Many people think of your department as offering courses in woodworking and mechanical drawing. How would you explain the changes in your department?
7. If you have twenty-one computer workstations and your class enrollment is twenty-four, how would you handle this situation?
8. What is meant by "tech prep"?
9. What industrial or business-related skills do you have to provide our students insight into how business operates?
10. What real-life skills will students develop from your department?
11. How can your department reach out to college bound students who do not enroll in your courses and provide them with experience in real-life skills?
12. What advice will you give your students relative to continuing their educational opportunities beyond high school?
13. How would your department establish a working relationship with community colleges and/or vocational schools, and what should that relationship be?
14. How would you react to a student who requested academic credit for actual apprentice experience taking place after school hours?
15. What steps do you take to impress on the students the importance of safety while using classroom equipment?

INTERVIEW NOTES FOR TEACHER: HOME AND CAREERS/HOME ECONOMICS

Interview Date   Candidate(s) Interviewed   Questions Used

Notes/Additional Questions

43

TEACHER: HOME AND CAREERS/HOME ECONOMICS

1. What are the current trends in family and consumer science?
2. How would you incorporate the use of computers in your department?
3. Many people think of your department as offering courses in cooking and sewing. How would you explain and clarify the philosophical changes that have taken place in your department?
4. If we were to offer a course primarily, but not exclusively, promoted to high school boys entitled "Single Living after High School," what kinds of lessons would you envision within the curriculum?
5. Please tell us about a project that could be undertaken by one of your classes at which the public was able to witness the activity.
6. How would you react if the drama department were to approach you and request assistance with costuming a production?
7. How would you react if requested to utilize the foods classes within a general building activity?
8. What career opportunities are available to students who enroll in your courses?
9. What steps would you take to impress on the students the importance of safety while using classroom equipment?
10. What are the primary areas for possible safety accidents in your department, and what steps would you take to minimize such possibilities?
11. What procedures would you follow should there be a student accident involving a hot appliance in your classroom?
12. Please talk to us about your vision of the ideal home and careers curriculum offerings in today's middle/high school.
13. When you perused our course offerings, what pros and cons did you discover?
14. Which students enroll for courses in your department, and how would you promote your department to increase enrollments?
15. Which courses do you feel most comfortable teaching?

INTERVIEW NOTES FOR GUIDANCE COUNSELOR

Interview Date   Candidate(s) Interviewed   Questions Used

Notes/Additional Questions

44

GUIDANCE COUNSELOR

1. What is the role of today's [*elementary/middle/high*] school guidance department?
2. Please give us three major concerns you have relating to guidance departments and how you would work to foster a positive response in these areas.
3. How can guidance counselors work with staff members who request assistance with student problems?
4. How would you deal with student problems yet maintain confidentiality?
5. Is there a point when a guidance counselor should negate confidentiality?
6. What is your accepted minimum ratio for the number of students to the number of guidance counselors in today's [*elementary/middle/high*] school?
7. How would you deal with an irate parent making allegations of incompetence against a teacher?
8. What is the proper involvement of parents in the guidance program?
9. What would you do to promote the guidance program to parents and to the public?
10. Guidance counsels work one-on-one in privacy. How do you provide for protection of the counselor against student allegations of inappropriate behavior during a conference behind closed doors?
11. Talk to us about the role of guidance counselors dealing with students who rank academically in the lower third of their class.
12. Have you had experience developing budgets for guidance programs?
13. In general, if you had to cut the guidance budget, where would you look to find the necessary cuts?
14. Please react to this hypothetical situation: You are the head of a K–12 guidance program that is very well balanced in staff, but you need to cut one position. Which grade level will it come from?
15. What procedure should guidance counselors follow to recommend colleges?
16. What is the responsibility of a guidance counselor if a student is determined to apply to a college that the guidance counselor believes is beyond the student's expectation?
17. The board of education informs you that they are not pleased that a number of students are being rejected from prestigious colleges. How do you react, and what do you tell them?
18. Students in our school tend to underestimate their ability for acceptance to prestigious colleges. What would you do to correct this impression?
19. How do you handle and schedule college representatives requesting to visit the high school?
20. What would you do to give students the opportunity to learn about careers in the trades?
21. What is your view of community college programs, and how would you present such programs to the students and their parents?
22. What qualities would you look for when hiring guidance counselors?

23. Should guidance counselors have classroom teaching experience before being hired for such a position?

24. Where and how does grief counseling fit into the responsibilities of the guidance program?

25. Classroom teachers often complain that vital student information is not provided to them. How would you handle such a complaint?

INTERVIEW NOTES FOR READING CONSULTANT

Interview Date   Candidate(s) Interviewed   Questions Used

Notes/Additional Questions

45

READING CONSULTANT

1. Please describe a guided reading lesson.
2. What recommendations would you give a classroom teacher who is uncooperative with the reading consultant?
3. Should parents have a role in their children's writing instruction?
4. How would you work with an experienced classroom teacher of several years who shows reluctance to your instructional initiatives?
5. What are your recommendations concerning classroom reading centers?
6. Please describe a balanced literacy program.
7. How would you implement a balanced literacy approach into the school's classrooms?
8. What expectations do you have for a teacher to determine the books that will be read to the students?
9. Are you experienced in developing a budget for your program?
10. How will you make reading materials available to teachers?
11. Which specific workshops have you conducted for teacher in-service training?
12. What are your expectations for our school library resources?
13. What is the role of the reading consultant as related to the library?
14. How will you work with parents who have concerns relative to specific books being used in the classroom?
15. How will you use technology in the school's reading program?

INTERVIEW NOTES FOR TEACHER: SPECIAL EDUCATION

Interview Date   Candidate(s) Interviewed   Questions Used

Notes/Additional Questions

46

TEACHER: SPECIAL EDUCATION

1. Please discuss your expectations of the general school population toward your special education class.
2. Please give us examples of how your classroom could be a full participant within the entire school setting.
3. What are your expectations of the special curriculum area programs, such as music and art, as related to your special education classroom?
4. What reading programs for a special education class composed of [*insert specifics*] are you most familiar with, and what are the pros and cons of the program?
5. Please discuss the writing process for a special education class composed of [*insert specifics*] and how you will use it in your classroom.
6. Please discuss a math lesson that you would teach for a special education class composed of [*insert specifics*].
7. Please give us an example of how you would use manipulatives in a special education math lesson for a class composed of [*insert specifics*].
8. Which tests would you use to conduct an educational evaluation of a child diagnosed with [*insert condition*] and why?
9. How would you integrate technology into your special education classroom?
10. Which specific areas of special education are you most comfortable teaching?
11. How would you utilize paraprofessionals or teacher assistants assigned to your classroom?
12. What qualities would you expect from paraprofessionals or teacher assistants assigned to your classroom?
13. Please describe a serious problem you encountered with a parent of a student assigned to your class, what position you took, and how the situation was resolved.
14. What is your opinion of the Individualized Educational Plan (IEP) process?
15. What steps could you take to better acquaint the general public about your program that, in turn, may lower the criticism of the cost associated with such programs?

INTERVIEW NOTES FOR TEACHER: ENGLISH AS A SECOND LANGUAGE (ESL)

Interview Date   Candidate(s) Interviewed   Questions Used

Notes/Additional Questions

47

TEACHER: ENGLISH AS A SECOND LANGUAGE (ESL)

1. Most ESL classes are to some extent multilevel. How would you handle large discrepancies in the ability levels of your students?
2. What is your opinion on the use of computers for ESL classes?
3. Computer skills are essential to ESL students, but the web, in particular, can be culturally difficult. How would you integrate computers and the Internet into your teaching?
4. What methods would you use to ensure equal talking time for all students?
5. How do you draw out the student who is reluctant to participate in talking time?
6. What ideas do you have for overcoming reluctance to write due to limited literacy in a first language?
7. How do you see your role as a teacher in discussions of culturally sensitive issues?
8. What procedures do you use when a new student enters your class?
9. How do you deal with students whose cultural background may cause the student to be intimidated by their new classroom surroundings?
10. Please tell us about a discipline problem you may have encountered in your ESL classroom that was unique to this student population and how you handled the situation.
11. What ideas do you have to assimilate your students into the entire school community?
12. What budget expectations would you have for an ESL program to be successful?
13. Talk to us about class size for this discipline.
14. Your class population is ever changing. How do you plan your program to accommodate such changes?
15. Do you use the arts as part of your ESL program, and, if so, how do you facilitate this?

INTERVIEW NOTES FOR TEACHER: LIBRARY/MEDIA RESOURCE CENTER

Interview Date   Candidate(s) Interviewed   Questions Used

Notes/Additional Questions

48

TEACHER: LIBRARY/MEDIA RESOURCE CENTER

1. Describe today's school library to a person who has not been in a school library since he or she graduated from high school twenty years ago.
2. Please tell us about the various components that comprise today's school library.
3. What relationship would you establish with the town library?
4. What state or regional sources are available to our library, and how would you utilize such services?
5. Have you ever developed a budget for a school library/media center?
6. Please describe how you would distribute the dollars in your budget to the various components of your program?
7. Which periodicals are today's school library expected to have on file for student use?
8. Which newspapers would you subscribe to for our library and why?
9. What safeguards can you take to prevent students from downloading inappropriate material from the computers in the center?
10. What steps would you take should you discover that a student has downloaded inappropriate material while using one of the center's computers?
11. Please describe your training in computers, relating that experience to your ability to assist students and faculty.
12. What procedures would you put into place for those persons who had concerns about a book in our library?
13. Are you familiar with any books that should not be placed in our school libraries?
14. How would you work with the faculty to increase the use of the school library?
15. Please describe the overall general climate we would find should we visit your library.

INTERVIEW NOTES FOR GENERAL QUESTIONS FOR ALL DISCIPLINES

Interview Date   Candidate(s) Interviewed   Questions Used

Notes/Additional Questions

49

GENERAL QUESTIONS FOR ALL DISCIPLINES

1. What is your responsibility in teaching traditional values to a child?
2. What do you consider to be a critical current issue in your discipline, and how will you address that issue as a teacher in our school district?
3. A student has failed three of the first four tests and shows little sign of effort to improve the situation. What steps would you take to remedy the problem?
4. Please tell us about a very successful lesson plan that you have used including the objective, what was achieved, and your assessment of the lesson.
5. How would you utilize a parent volunteer?
6. What instructional strategies do you use that help create a culture for learning?
7. What do you see as the most critical element in a successful teacher?
8. Describe how you would involve your students in the learning process.
9. What strategies would you employ with the "low-motivated" student?
10. What strategies would you employ to keep the high achiever stimulated?
11. What methods of feedback do you provide students and parents?
12. Have you ever used e-mail to communicate with parents?
13. What experience do you have with adviser–advisee, exploratory, flexible block scheduling, and looping?
14. What contributions to our school could we expect if you were to join our staff?
15. If a student were to approach you and ask for a recommendation of how to prepare to be a teacher in your discipline, what advice would you give that student?
16. A student informs you that she would like to take a particular course in your department but cannot fit it into the schedule. What would you do to assist and/or accommodate that student?
17. Research indicates that there are four "learning styles." Do you take learning styles into consideration when developing lessons, tests, and assignments? If not, why would you not take this into account? If yes, describe how you address learning styles.
18. If I visit your class, describe what I would see during a forty-five-minute lesson.
19. In regard to Bloom's taxonomy, identify higher-order thinking skills. Please explain and give examples of ways in which you would teach these skills.
20. Where do you see yourself in five years?

INTERVIEW NOTES FOR THE FIRST-YEAR TEACHER

Interview Date   Candidate(s) Interviewed   Questions Used

Notes/Additional Questions

50

THE FIRST-YEAR TEACHER

1. Tell us about your student teaching experience.
2. What were you not prepared for when you began student teaching?
3. Please describe a lesson plan that really worked for you.
4. Please discuss a lesson plan that did not work and why.
5. What college course best prepared you to be a teacher?
6. What advice proved to be very important as you began student teaching?
7. Were you assigned any duties in your student teaching school?
8. What was your most challenging student discipline experience, and how did you handle it?
9. Give yourself a grade on how you handled student discipline, and explain why.
10. How will you improve your handling of student discipline?
11. Did you have an opportunity to work with various ethnic populations?
12. How would you describe your level of friendship with the students?
13. Did you have an opportunity to work with students in any school activities?
14. Did you have an opportunity to work with other staff members?
15. Tell us about your interaction with other teachers in the building.
16. You learned how to write a lesson plan in college. With student teaching behind you, how has that planning changed?
17. Did you have an opportunity to discuss your experiences with the building principal or assistant principal?
18. Which discipline did you feel most comfortable teaching?
19. Which discipline did you feel least comfortable teaching?
20. How did you handle grading of student work?
21. Did you have an opportunity to take students on a field trip as part of your student teaching?
22. Tell us about you interaction with parents.
23. Discuss a conference you may have had with a parent concerning a student.
24. As you listen to your college colleagues describe their student teaching, how do you feel about your own experience and your capability?
25. Looking back at your total student teaching experience, what would you do differently?

INTERVIEW NOTES FOR CLASSROOM MANAGEMENT

Interview Date   Candidate(s) Interviewed   Questions Used

Notes/Additional Questions

51

CLASSROOM MANAGEMENT

1. How would you describe the effectiveness of your classroom management?
2. Please talk to us about your style of classroom management.
3. What approaches do you use to manage classroom behavior?
4. How would you adjust your classroom management for various levels of learners?
5. Do you believe in the use of rewards for classroom management?
6. Please tell us about reward systems you have used for classroom management.
7. What has your experience been concerning detentions?
8. Have you found any negative aspects to student detentions?
9. At what point is a student detention necessary?
10. Do you ever postpone a student detention due to the student's unavailability on the day of the infraction that made the detention necessary?
11. Would you postpone a student detention if that student had a school activity or athletic event that was occurring at the same time?
12. What is your opinion of central detention where the duty is rotated among the teaching staff?
13. What is your next recourse when detentions no longer work?
14. At what point in the discipline procedure do you involve an administrator?
15. Please tell us the details of an incident when you determined it necessary to send a student to the office due to discipline.
16. What is your minimum expectation when you send a student to the office for disciplinary reasons?
17. What steps would you take should you send a student to the office for disciplinary reasons and the outcome does not meet your expectation?
18. How often have you found it necessary to send a student to the office for disciplinary reasons?
19. Please tell us about a disciplinary measure that forced you to send the student to the office only to be dissatisfied with the action taken by the administrator.
20. At what point do you involve the parents in a student discipline problem?
21. Please tell us about a meeting with parents concerning their child's discipline and the outcome.
22. What steps would you take if a parent refused to attend a meeting to discuss the child's discipline?
23. Please tell us why you believe your method of classroom management works.
24. Is there any relationship to your grading procedures and the student's disruptive classroom behavior?
25. Has an administrator ever had to work with you to improve your discipline tactics?

INTERVIEW NOTES FOR SOCIAL WORKER

Interview Date   Candidate(s) Interviewed   Questions Used

Notes/Additional Questions

52

SOCIAL WORKER

1. Please elaborate on your social work experience with children.
2. What are three of the most critical areas we need to be aware of pertaining to children in an [*elementary/middle/high*] school setting?
3. Which student age levels are you most comfortable working with?
4. What are some common concerns relative to referrals?
5. How would you handle an anonymous referral?
6. How do you handle "need-to-know" information?
7. Classroom teachers often complain that vital student information is not provided to them. How would you handle such a complaint?
8. Have you had experience with pupil placement team (PPT) meetings?
9. What are the positive and negative aspects of PPT meetings?
10. How do you deal with parents who are unwilling to work with you?
11. How do you deal with parents who are not willing to acknowledge that a problem may exist?
12. Please give us an example of a difficult case study you have managed and how you handled it.
13. Please give us an example of a case study you have managed that did not have a favorable outcome and why.
14. How will you adjust your schedule to accommodate your case assignments?
15. Do you ever have personal fears doing this sort of work? If so, please give us an example and how you strive to overcome the fear.

INTERVIEW NOTES FOR SCHOOL NURSE

Interview Date   Candidate(s) Interviewed   Questions Used

Notes/Additional Questions

53

SCHOOL NURSE

1. What age level of student are you most comfortable working with?
2. What experience have you had in nursing as related to children?
3. Do you hold valid nursing licenses?
4. How do you deal with the chronically ill student?
5. At what point do you tell a student that he or she is fine and to go back to class?
6. Should teachers screen students who have a health complaint?
7. What procedures would you put in place to dispense student medications?
8. If you were asked to present a workshop for teachers, what material would you determine essential to cover?
9. How much information would you keep on file concerning a student's health?
10. How would you handle student requests for birth control information?
11. What experience have you had dealing with students who have problems with drug dependency?
12. Have you had experience dealing with students who sustain athletic injuries?
13. What is the typical schedule for a school nurse?
14. This position requires services at [*insert number*] schools. How do you handle such a situation when most of the student problems occur in the morning hours?
15. Would you please share with us a difficult situation in your professional career you had to deal with and how you handled it?

INTERVIEW NOTES FOR PARAPROFESSIONAL/TEACHER ASSISTANT

Interview Date   Candidate(s) Interviewed   Questions Used

Notes/Additional Questions

54

PARAPROFESSIONAL/ TEACHER ASSISTANT

1. Have you ever worked in an actual school classroom setting?
2. Have you ever worked with young people in a church group, youth athletics, scouting, or similar settings?
3. Have you ever worked with young people with special needs?
4. What do you believe is the role of a paraprofessional?
5. Have you ever spoken with anyone who is or has been a paraprofessional, and, if so, what has that person told you about this kind of position?
6. Why do you believe you are qualified for this kind of position?
7. If selected, you would be living and working in the same community. How would you deal with issues of confidentiality?
8. What do you view as the difference between teaching and reinforcing of material?
9. What special skills do you have that would aid us in properly placing you in a paraprofessional position?
10. What is the highest grade level of [*insert grade and subject—e.g., math, reading*] at which you would feel comfortable working?
11. Do you have any craft skills that could be used to assist the teacher in such things as class projects, plays, or decorating bulletin boards?
12. This position involves working with [*insert job characteristics*]. How do you see yourself working in this type of situation?
13. This position involves working with [*insert job characteristics*]. Why do you believe you are qualified for this type of assignment?
14. This position involves working with [*insert job characteristics*] and can be difficult for some people to handle emotionally. How would you cope with these kinds of issues?
15. Should there be an emergency or unexpected event, you may find yourself in charge of a group of students in a classroom or even on a field trip. Do you have any concerns in your ability if this sort of assignment is given to you?

INTERVIEW NOTES FOR SUBSTITUTE TEACHER

Interview Date   Candidate(s) Interviewed   Questions Used

Notes/Additional Questions

55

SUBSTITUTE TEACHER

1. Why do you want to be a substitute teacher?
2. Do you have aspirations of becoming a teacher?
3. Had you ever considered becoming a teacher?
4. Have you had any teaching experience?
5. What experience have you had working with children?
6. Which grade level would you be comfortable teaching?
7. Which subjects would you be comfortable teaching?
8. Are there subjects you would not consider teaching?
9. Would you substitute in areas such as music, art, or physical education?
10. Do you have restrictions on working hours or days?
11. What is your highest level of formal education?
12. What was your major in college?
13. Have you had experience with home schooling?
14. What excites you the most about being a substitute teacher?
15. What frightens you the most about being a substitute teacher?

INTERVIEW NOTES FOR COACH

Interview Date   Candidate(s) Interviewed   Questions Used

Notes/Additional Questions

56

COACH

1. What is the extent of your athletic experience both as a player and as a coach?
2. What is your background in caring for sports injuries?
3. Talk to us about your philosophy of tryouts and cutting as a result of the tryout.
4. How do you work with the student and parent when they disagree with how you cut players?
5. Describe your philosophy of winning.
6. What advice will you give students who ask for information concerning nutritional supplements?
7. What is your position on the use of steroids by student athletes?
8. Have you had to deal with a student who has abused drugs to enhance performance, and, if so, how did you handle the situation?
9. You will be following in the footsteps of a winning coach who is retiring. How do you approach this position?
10. This is a new sport for our school. How do you recruit players?
11. One of your athletes informs you that a teacher is treating her unfairly, and her grade in that class may prevent further athletic participation. What would you tell the student, and would you follow up on this in any way?
12. You are a male coaching a female sport. How do you handle this situation?
13. Please tell us about a difficult situation you faced as a coach—how you handled it and what the outcome was.
14. You will be coaching [*insert sport*], and weight is always a major factor and often raises criticism. Talk to us about your expectations with these situations.
15. Coaches often become parent figures and are asked for personal advice. How would you handle such situations?

INTERVIEW NOTES FOR SECURITY OFFICER

Interview Date   Candidate(s) Interviewed   Questions Used

Notes/Additional Questions

57

SECURITY OFFICER

1. Please tell us about all of your experiences related to this kind of work.
2. Have you ever worked in a school setting?
3. How do you view the role of a school security officer?
4. What have you heard about the climate of our school?
5. How long has it been since you were last in a high school, and how do you think that setting has changed in that amount of time?
6. What training have you had in any of the martial arts?
7. Have you had any experience with metal detectors and/or visual monitors?
8. Have you had any experience with drug enforcement?
9. What is your experience with recognizing drugs?
10. Have you had training to recognize drugs?
11. Please talk to us about when to use force.
12. Please tell us about a situation you encountered in your previous security position in which you found it necessary to use force.
13. Have you had any experience in mediation techniques?
14. What kinds of things would you be looking for if assigned to security duty at a night football game?
15. This position may require evening and weekend work for such things as dances and athletic events. How visible should security be at such events?

INTERVIEW NOTES FOR SECRETARY

Interview Date   Candidate(s) Interviewed   Questions Used

Notes/Additional Questions

58

SECRETARY

1. What previous secretarial experience have you had that would be of benefit to the position you are seeking?
2. Why do you wish to use your secretarial skills in a school setting?
3. Please tell us about your experiences if you have ever worked or volunteered in a school.
4. A secretary has a great deal of interaction with students of all ages. Please tell us about your experiences working with children in settings such as religious, scouting, or similar youth groups.
5. How do you envision a typical day in the life of a school secretary at the [*elementary/middle/high*] school level?
6. Do you consider yourself an organized person?
7. Are you a flexible person? If so, please give us an example of how you handle change.
8. Have you worked in a position where you have had to deal with the general public?
9. How do you believe you would respond to an irate parent making demands of you while visiting the school office?
10. Have you had experience handling confidential documents?
11. Which computer programs are you able to use, and what is your competency level in each of these programs?
12. Do you take dictation?
13. Have you had experience with any kind of bookkeeping functions?
14. Please share with us a negative experience you had in a previous position—how you handled it and what the outcome was.
15. I'm going to give you a handwritten memo similar to one the principal may give you to prepare in an office. Before leaving today, please use the computer in the outer office and provide us with a finished document of this memo. [*Note*: The draft document should contain one or two spelling errors, some words that are difficult to read, and other such aspects. You will be able to determine the candidate's ability to use a computer, how long the assignment took to complete, and examine the finished document.]

INTERVIEW NOTES FOR CUSTODIAN

Interview Date   Candidate(s) Interviewed   Questions Used

Notes/Additional Questions

59

CUSTODIAN

1. Please tell us about your previous employment in the custodial area.
2. Have you ever worked in a school setting?
3. Why do you want to use your skills in a school setting?
4. What kinds of cleaning materials should be avoided and not found in schools?
5. What are some hazardous cleaning materials that could be found in our schools?
6. What are some typical sources of asbestos in old buildings?
7. Children in elementary schools, and also in some special classes at all levels, can and will have personal hygiene accidents. Do you have any difficulty with cleaning in such situations?
8. Are you a flexible person?
9. Requests for custodial services may come from many people in a school. For example, it may be the principal, the teacher, or the cafeteria staff. Do you consider yourself a flexible person, and how do you think you would respond to such unplanned work requests?
10. Do you have any special qualifications in any of the trades?
11. Are you capable of making minor or temporary repairs in carpentry, plumbing, and electrical situations?
12. Are you qualified to service swimming pools?
13. What would you do if you observed a student—or, for that matter, a teacher—damaging school property?
14. If you found that a certain classroom is always dirtier than other rooms at the end of each day, how would you handle the situation?
15. What special requests would you make to the staff as the building's custodian?

INTERVIEW NOTES FOR PARENT VOLUNTEER

Interview Date   Candidate(s) Interviewed   Questions Used

Notes/Additional Questions

60

PARENT VOLUNTEER

1. Please share with us why you wish to be a parent volunteer.
2. What do you know about our schools?
3. Have you ever worked with children in a religious, scouting, or similar youth group setting?
4. Your child is a student in this school. Do you see this as a conflict of interest?
5. Your child is a student in this school. How do you think your child will react to your presence in the building?
6. Would you be willing to be assigned as a volunteer in another school within our district where you do not have children enrolled?
7. A major concern we have with volunteers, and employees alike, is confidentiality. How will you handle confidentiality relative to your observations after you leave the building for the day?
8. Do you have any special area of interest in which you would like to spend your time with us?
9. Do you have any special skills that would lend themselves to your volunteer work?
10. If a teacher needed assistance in the classroom, are there any academic areas that you feel more comfortable working in than others?
11. Please share with us a previous difficult experience in your volunteer work and how you handled it.
12. Would you be willing to accompany students on field trips?
13. Are there any kinds of duties you would not accept?
14. What are your computer skills?
15. Here is a book suitable for a grade 2 student. Please pretend that we are second graders and read to us in the manner you would if you were in a classroom.

Notes/Additional Questions

61

ILLEGAL APPLICATION AND INTERVIEW QUESTIONS

1. How old are you?
2. What year did you graduate from high school/college?
3. What country were you born in?
4. What is your race?
5. What religion do you practice?
6. What is your sex?
7. Will you send us a photograph of yourself?
8. What is your sexual preference?
9. What is your marital status?
10. What are your marital plans?
11. What are your plans for raising a family?
12. What medical conditions or diseases have you been treated for?
13. What medical conditions have caused you to be hospitalized?
14. Have you ever been treated for a mental condition?
15. How many days were you absent from work due to illness last year?
16. Is there any health-related reason you may not be able to perform the job for which you are applying?
17. Have you ever been treated for drug addiction?
18. Have you ever been treated for alcoholism?
19. Do you have any physical defects or disabilities that would prohibit you from performing certain kinds of work?
20. Have you ever filed for workers' compensation?

ABOUT THE AUTHOR

William L. Gagnon Jr. received a bachelor of music degree from Boston University, a master of arts from the University of Connecticut, and a Sixth Year Professional Diploma in School Administration and Supervision from Southern Connecticut State University. His professional career in public school education spanned thirty-eight years. He taught all aspects of high school music for twenty-four years at The Morgan School in Clinton, Connecticut, where the school auditorium is named in his honor. He also served as that school district's music coordinator K–12. He subsequently served as supervisor of fine arts K–12 and as director of personnel for the Hicksville, New York, public schools and as director of human resources and administration for the East Hartford, Connecticut, public schools.

Mr. Gagnon is a past president of the Connecticut Association of School Personnel Administrators. He retired in 1998 and now works part-time as an educational and human resources consultant. Mr. Gagnon resides with his wife, Barbara, in Madison, Connecticut.